ALSO BY RICHARD MAURER

Destination Moon:
The Remarkable and Improbable Voyage of Apollo 11

The Wright Sister: Katharine Wright and Her Famous Brothers

RICHARD MAURER

THE WOMAN IN THE MOON

How Margaret Hamilton Helped Fly the First Astronauts to the Moon

ROARING BROOK PRESS

NEW YORK

Published by Roaring Brook Press
Roaring Brook Press is a division of
Holtzbrinck Publishing Holdings Limited Partnership
120 Broadway, New York, NY 10271 • mackids.com

Our books may be purchased in bulk for promotional, educational, or business use.
Please contact your local bookseller or the Macmillan Corporate and
Premium Sales Department at (800) 221-7945 ext. 5442 or by email at
MacmillanSpecialMarkets@macmillan.com.

Library of Congress Cataloging-in-Publication Data
Names: Maurer, Richard, 1950– author.
Title: The woman in the moon : how Margaret Hamilton helped fly
the first astronauts to the moon / Richard Maurer.
Description: First edition. | New York, NY : Roaring Brook Press, 2023. |
Includes bibliographical references and index. | Audience: Ages 10–14 |
Audience: Grades 7–9 | Summary: "A stunning and intimate biography of
Margaret Hamilton, the computer engineer who helped Apollo 11 and mankind get
from the Earth to the Moon." —Provided by publisher.
Identifiers: LCCN 2022029750 | ISBN 9781626728561 (hardcover) |
ISBN 9781626728578 (ebook)
Subjects: LCSH: Hamilton, Margaret Heafield, 1936– —Juvenile literature. | Computer
software developers—United States—Biography—Juvenile literature. | Computer
programmers—United States—Biography—Juvenile literature. | Women scientists—United
States—Biography—Juvenile literature. | Scientists—United States—Biography—Juvenile
literature. | Project Apollo (U.S.)—History—Juvenile literature. | Moon—Juvenile literature. |
United States. National Aeronautics and Space Administration—Officials and
employees—Biography—Juvenile literature.
Classification: LCC QA76.2.H36 M38 2023 | DDC 005.1092—dc23/eng/20221109
LC record available at https://lccn.loc.gov/2022029750

First edition, 2023
Book design by Veronica Mang
Printed in the United States of America by Lakeside Book Company,
Harrisonburg, Virginia

1   3   5   7   9   10   8   6   4   2

To Alex, Rowan, and Olive

Margaret Hamilton and the code that sent humans to the Moon.

CONTENTS

Prologue: Men Only xi

PART 1: GROWING UP 1

1.   The Upper Peninsula. 3

     Women in the Moon 9

2.   Asking Questions 13

3.   The Banana Mine 21

4.   College Woman. 29

5.   Earlham. 35

6.   Math, Philosophy, and Religion 41

     Charlotte Angas Scott 46

7.   The Cold Warrior 49

8.   Jim. 55

9.   Thinking Machines. 61

     The ENIAC Women 67

10. The Weather Man. 71

     The Butterfly Effect. 79

11. Two New Computers 83

PART 2: COUNTDOWN 91

12. The Ad 93

13. The AGC 99

     Doc Gets the Job 103

14. The Program 107

    Ada, Countess of Lovelace 115

15. The IL. 119

16. FORGET IT 125

17. The Astronauts Versus the AGC .131

18. "What If . . . ?" 137

    Katherine Johnson 143

19. The Bug Detective 147

20. Black Friday 153

21. The Fire. 159

22. Kenneth. 165

PART 3: TO THE MOON 171

23. Apollo 8. 173

24. The Lauren Bug 181

    The Other Onboard Computer 186

25. Apollo 11. 191

26. Never-Supposed-to-Happen Alarms 199

27. Computer "Error" 207

28. "Wake Up, Margaret!" 215

    Acknowledgments. 223

    Margaret Hamilton Time Line 227

    Notes. 229

    References 239

    Image Credits 248

    Index 249

She was the Goddess of Software.

—Hugh Blair-Smith, software engineer

Space travelers take sightings
from the Moon near their crashed
ship in Jules Verne's 1869 novel
A Trip Around the Moon.

MEN ONLY

ONE EVENING IN THE LATE 1950s, MASSACHUSETTS senator John F. Kennedy and his brother Robert were enjoying a relaxing dinner with their companion, a brilliant, eccentric inventor named Charles Stark "Doc" Draper. Doc was trying to sell Jack and Bobby on the idea of space travel. It was more than idle talk since Jack was planning to run for president and might soon have the power to do something about Doc's advice. To Doc, spaceflight was serious business. America's most powerful rival, the Soviet Union, had recently launched the world's first artificial satellite, a radio transmitter that circled the Earth every ninety-six minutes. Humans would inevitably follow, Doc believed. He further maintained that one day people would ride rockets to the Moon and even beyond, and he felt that the country could not afford to fall behind in this vital technology. He even offered to help, since his research lab at the Massachusetts Institute of Technology was working on the problem of navigating across the chartless realm of space, which was one of the most difficult problems of space travel.

Doc's call to action was taking place at Boston's exclusive Locke-Ober Café, a men-only establishment that sported wood paneling, hearty but elegant food, a well-stocked bar, and a painting of a scantily clad woman, just like in an Old West saloon. Locke-Ober was the ideal place for male executives to get together to make deals. Doc had hoped he could light a spark in the Kennedy brothers that might flare into something significant. But somewhere between drinks and dessert, the deal fizzled. Jack and Bobby listened politely, but with growing irritation. As Doc later lamented, they "could not be convinced that all rockets were not a waste of money, and space navigation even worse."

• • •

Jump ahead to May 25, 1961. Jack Kennedy was now president of the United States and addressing a joint session of Congress. In 1961,

Doc Draper lectures on engineering.

President John F. Kennedy signs a bill. Directly behind him is his brother Attorney General Robert F. Kennedy.

Congress was a lot like Locke-Ober. Of the more than five hundred senators and representatives, only twenty were women. Among the country's urgent needs, the president listed the very subject broached by Doc that earlier evening at Locke-Ober.

"I believe that this nation should commit itself to achieving the goal, before this decade is out," President Kennedy proclaimed, "of landing a man on the moon and returning him safely to the earth."

What had changed his mind? The United States had fallen farther behind the Soviet Union in space, and it was imperative that the nation do something dramatic to catch up. The assembled legislators were stunned at the boldness of Kennedy's proposal.

The president went on, "No single space project in this period will be more impressive to mankind, or more important for the long-range exploration of space; and none will be so difficult or expensive to accomplish."

He was right about the expense. According to some estimates, the Moon-landing program would cost $40 billion, almost as much as the entire U.S. defense budget in 1961. He was also right about the difficulty, since the hardware to send people to the Moon didn't exist yet—not the rockets, not the spacecraft, not the launch facilities, not the control centers, not the tracking stations, and not the guidance system, which was Doc's specialty.

Doc was as surprised as he was pleased by Kennedy's announcement. Furthermore, he was ready. Just eleven weeks later, on August 10, 1961, his MIT Instrumentation Lab signed the first major contract awarded for Project Apollo, which was the name of the Moon venture. The lab's assignment was to create a truly astonishing device: a miniature computer that would travel to the Moon with the astronauts, unerringly guiding them there and back. Nothing like it had ever been built, and many experts believed it couldn't be done.

Boston's Locke-Ober Café during its men-only era.
Note the painting on the far wall.

• • •

A few years later, Doc's Apollo Guidance Computer was fully designed, and his specialists were deep into writing the AGC's code, the onboard flight software. This was the set of instructions that would make the computer do what Doc had promised. Gatherings at Locke-Ober were frequent, since that was where Doc liked to entertain his staff and visitors—all male, of course. On one particular evening, the party included astronauts from the space center in Houston. Doc couldn't attend, but the hosts that night were his engineers. In those days, computers filled entire rooms, consumed enormous amounts of electricity, ran code on heavy trays of punched cards, and broke down frequently. But the AGC was the size of a suitcase, consumed the power of a lightbulb, had its software entirely wired in, and would never fail. At least, that was the idea.

The astronauts were not so sure. Over dinner in one of Locke-Ober's private rooms, they let the MIT team know how skeptical they were. Most of the astronauts were test pilots, and they were not shy about airing their objections. Proud of their ability to fly the fastest and most dangerous jets of the day, they were concerned that normal piloting functions on the lunar voyage would be handled mostly by the AGC and the onboard flight software. Indeed, that was the plan. To fire a rocket, the astronauts would have to enter a command into an electronic display. Landing on the Moon would be entirely automated unless they intervened. So would reentering Earth's atmosphere. The Moon landing and reentry were two of the most perilous parts of the mission, and the astronauts didn't like the idea of staking their lives on what they sarcastically called a "thinking machine."

The astronauts could be outspoken, inflexible, and blunt. One liked to say, only half-jokingly, "Of course, we'll shut the computer off as soon as we're up there."

But Doc's engineers were just as impassioned, if more polite. They insisted that this was the only way to get to the Moon on President Kennedy's deadline. "Before this decade is out," the president had said. In other words, by the end of 1969, which was just a few years away. The MIT team noted that there were too many steps in the mission, too little fuel, and almost no tolerance for error. Computer control gave Apollo its only chance for success.

Refusing to give in, one of the astronauts liked to point out that engineers at the plant where the Moon lander was being built had warned that computer control would never work and that the idea was "crazy."

• • •

On it went, back and forth, over Locke-Ober's calorie-laden dishes and potent drinks, as the scantily clad lady in the painting downstairs held her wine cup eternally aloft. Under other circumstances, the astronauts might have gotten their way. But the space agency had decreed that the spacemen could suggest changes; however, they could not alter the decision to fly to the Moon using an ambitious, risky, and untried computer and its software.

Through the loud voices and clouds of tobacco smoke, it might have been any meeting of high-powered businessmen at the time—with one big difference. On this particular evening there was a woman present. Remarkably, the restaurant staff had not asked her to leave. In fact, she was a key member of the MIT team. Equally accomplished as her male colleagues, she was quieter than they were, though no less self-assured. She was one of the top engineers working on the code that would make Apollo's computer do what the astronauts seemed to dread. In her forthright and unpretentious way, she would help ensure the success of Project Apollo.

Who was she?

The Upper and Lower
Peninsulas of Michigan, 1894.

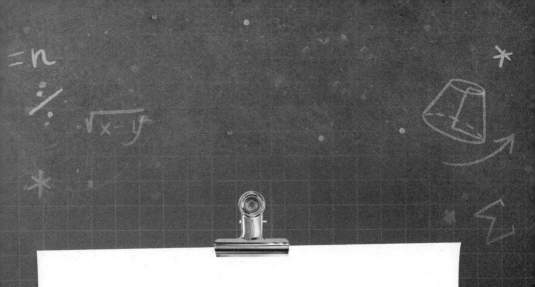

PART 1

GROWING UP

Margaret "Bunny" Heafield (later Margaret Hamilton), on her second birthday.

CHAPTER 1

THE UPPER PENINSULA

FROM AGE TEN, MARGARET HAMILTON LIVED IN A place that might as well have been the Moon to most Americans. The Upper Peninsula of Michigan is a vast, sparsely populated woodland one fourth the size of Florida. Shaped like the head of a long-beaked bird, it is bordered by three of the five Great Lakes—on the north by Lake Superior and on the south by Lakes Michigan and Huron. Across the water to the south is Michigan's Lower Peninsula, shaped like a giant mitten, which is where most of the state's people live.

The Lower Peninsula is famous for its industry, principally the giant automobile plants in the state's largest city, Detroit. The Upper Peninsula—or U.P., as locals call it—is renowned for its unspoiled beauty, its mineral deposits, and the harshest winters in the United States, with some places averaging nearly twenty feet of snow annually.

• • •

She was born Margaret Elaine Heafield (pronounced "hayfield") to Esther and Kenneth Heafield in Paoli, Indiana, on August 17, 1936.

Clearing snow from the railroad during a typical northern Michigan winter.

As a child, Margaret got the nickname Bunny. She would stay Bunny until she was an adult and landed a university job where there was another woman named Bunny. Since that Bunny had seniority, Margaret used her given name from then on.

Both of Margaret's parents were teachers, and they moved around the Midwest for several years before finally returning to the U.P., where Kenneth had grown up. Moving around was a tradition with the Heafields, since Kenneth had been born in England before emigrating first to Canada and then to Michigan with his parents.

Margaret's earliest years coincided with the Great Depression, which was a worldwide economic crisis that lasted throughout the 1930s. At its worst, the Depression left up to a quarter of the U.S. workforce unemployed. Luckily, teachers could usually find jobs if they were willing to move. So every year or two young Margaret ended up in a different town, as Kenneth and Esther shifted between poorly paid, temporary positions.

The Great Depression was followed by another national crisis, World War II, which America entered when Margaret was five years old. Like many young men, Kenneth joined the military and was shipped overseas. This was an even more chaotic time than usual for the family, since Margaret and her brother and sister were often split up, living with their grandparents in Indiana or their mother, wherever she happened to be teaching.

A few days before her ninth birthday in the summer of 1945, Margaret and her friends were reenacting a children's book about finding an upside-down country on the other side of the world. They were digging a hole to get there when suddenly all the bells in town started

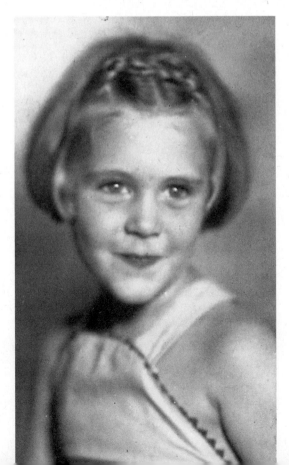

Margaret, about age four.

ringing and every car horn began tooting. Had they broken through? Were they in trouble?

No, the war had ended.

Things settled down after that. Kenneth returned, and the family moved to Sault Ste. Marie in the U.P., where he took a job as an English professor at a branch of the Michigan College of Mining and Technology. Esther and Kenneth had another baby—a boy—completing their family with two girls and two boys. As the oldest child, Margaret was often given adult responsibilities.

She was now in elementary school and could finally put down roots. Through high school, she would live in only two towns, both in the U.P.

• • •

For a young person, the Upper Peninsula was a never-ending adventure, with ghost towns, abandoned mines, old forts, vast forests, and miles and miles of lakeshore. When not in school, Margaret and her siblings played outside—summer and winter—until her mother rang a big cowbell that could be heard from far away, signaling that dinner was ready. Margaret later recalled that she and her brothers and sister grew up "like weeds," meaning they were untended and left free to develop on their own.

Margaret loved searching for arrowheads in the places where American Indians had hunted and lived during the thousands of years they occupied the U.P. Aside from the wealth of fish and game, one reason they came was for the native copper—pure metallic copper that could be chipped out of rock, heated, and easily fashioned into projectile points, knives, fishing hooks, and other tools. These

The Pictured Rocks region in the Upper Peninsula of Michigan.

earlier inhabitants could not have known, but they had discovered the largest deposits of native copper in the entire world, which explains why the Michigan College of Mining and Technology later opened in the region.

American Indians had another connection to the U.P.—at least in the minds of millions of schoolchildren. The peninsula was the setting for a long poem that children all over the country had to memorize, in part, and recite. First published in 1855, *The Song of Hiawatha* by Henry Wadsworth Longfellow is based on American Indian lore and tells the story of the Ojibwa warrior Hiawatha: how he grew up "on the shores of Gitche Gumee," or Lake Superior; how he battled monsters, sorcerers, and nature spirits; and how he and his beautiful bride, Minnehaha, were honored with a magnificent wedding feast. The story is set amid the U.P.'s dark forests, rushing rivers, plunging chasms, and overarching canopy of sky, Sun, Moon, and stars.

The verses children had to learn included a passage where Hiawatha hears the origin of the human figure that is visible in the full Moon:

> *"Once a warrior, very angry,*
> *Seized his grandmother, and threw her*
> *Up into the sky at midnight;*
> *Right against the moon he threw her;*
> *'T is her body that you see there."*

This episode explains the shape that many people see in the Moon's dark regions. Some describe the form as a man or even a rabbit. However, in the poem it is a woman, and Hiawatha is her great-grandson. To those who heard the legend centuries ago, it made sense that a great hero on Earth should be related to the inhabitant of the most impressive object in the night sky. That a human might be propelled to the Moon made perfect sense—at least in a story.

The Woman in the Moon, from a tattoo pattern of the Haida people in Northwest America.

WOMEN IN THE MOON

No one can look at the Sun for more than an instant, but the Moon is endlessly viewable. Even without a telescope, it presents a gloriously changing spectacle—from a graceful crescent, resembling the tip of a fingernail, to the brilliance of a full Moon, blazing like a searchlight. Little wonder that this entrancing globe has inspired countless stories, especially because the variation of light and dark areas on the Moon suggests different shapes: a man, a rabbit, a frog, a woman.

In ancient Greece, one legend described the figure in the Moon as the Sibyl of Delphi, a soothsayer who died and ascended to the lunar realm, where she flies

Can you find the Woman in the Moon?

Jean-Dominique Cassini's telescopic map of the Moon, 1679. The square shows the location of the Moon Maiden (see close-up on the next page).

around uttering prophecies. Any space travelers in the vicinity may overhear and thereby know the future.

To the Alutiiq people of Kodiak Island in what is now Alaska, the shape is a mask, shared between a husband and wife. For two weeks, the man wears the mask as the Moon grows from a crescent phase to full. Then his wife takes over, shrinking from full Moon back to a thin crescent.

With the invention of the telescope in 1608, observers could at last see the true nature of the Moon, discovering that it is a world of mountains, valleys, plains, and craters. The dark areas are plains (early mapmakers mistook them for seas). The light areas are mountains. Still, the instinct to discern a face did not go away. In the 1670s the French astronomer Jean-Dominique Cassini produced the most detailed lunar map of his day. On it, at a point of land at the edge of what is called the Bay of Rainbows, Cassini placed the exquisitely rendered head of a woman, with her hair flowing out into the Sea of Rains.

No one knows for sure who she is. But like the other women in the Moon, she lives on in that glowing orb.

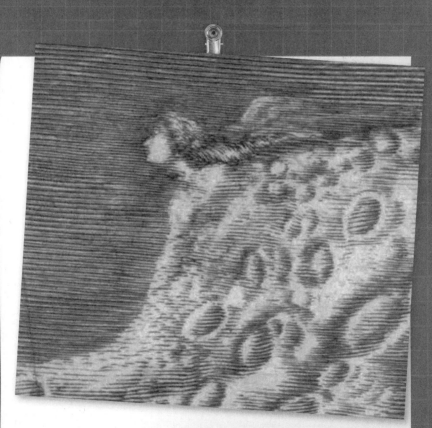

Cassini's Moon Maiden. Officially called the Promontorium Heraclides, the formation resembles the head of a woman under certain lighting conditions.

Margaret in high school.

CHAPTER 2
ASKING QUESTIONS

RESIDENTS OF THE U.P. SOMETIMES FELT FORGOT-
ten by the rest of the country. No one passed through the region
on the way to somewhere else. There were no major industries.
In 1950, the U.P. had no television stations and no big airports.
There were scattered public libraries, plus a few small colleges
like the one where Kenneth worked. Larger towns usually had a
movie theater. But there was precious little that might be considered entertainment or enrichment. Some would even say the U.P.
was boring.

But when you grow up in a boring place, you learn never to be
bored. For one thing, the U.P. had natural beauty galore, which was
on display whenever the Heafields made their long drives to see relatives. On the way to Margaret's grandmother's house in Garden,
Michigan, they passed through the Hiawatha National Forest, before
emerging onto the Garden Peninsula with its spectacular view down
Lake Michigan, where ships could sometimes be seen in the distance
carrying cargo from Chicago, Milwaukee, and other busy ports to the
south.

On these trips, Margaret played games with her siblings, sang songs, or just thought about things: the woods, the lake, the ships, the fact that the car could break down at any minute (which it often did). Or how she might be imagining all of this.

"Do you suppose that we're just dreaming now—that we're not really here?" she might ask her father, who was driving.

Some parents would have replied, "Where did you get that idea?" Or, "Don't be ridiculous!"

However, Kenneth always had a thoughtful response, "Now *that* is interesting!" he might say. "You know, I've sometimes thought that too."

Kenneth taught English, but he was a philosopher at heart. He took Margaret's questions seriously and treated her like an adult. Maybe she didn't know as much as he did, but that was only because he was older. Aside from their age difference, he considered her an equal.

Margaret's mother, Esther, was more traditional and practical. Above all, she was down-to-earth, and she teased Margaret about having her head in the clouds—which was true. Margaret loved nothing so much as discussing ideas with her dad. Asking questions and searching for answers was her entertainment—and education.

Aside from philosophy, another of Kenneth's passions was poetry, which he would recite from memory on their drives: Shakespeare, Lord Byron, John Keats, Emily Dickinson. These were some of the authors he taught his students. An avid poet himself, he enjoyed writing on philosophical themes, like this stanza from a poem about a train journey, in which he recounts the type of questions Margaret would pose on their drives:

Is this for certain the way things go?

What comes after the rain and the snow?

Are you and I the travelers tonight

Riding this train and talking so bright?

Or is it a dream? What would you say?

Do you think it might be a story too good to stay?

• • •

Margaret grew up with poetry and philosophy—especially if you consider religion to be philosophy. Both of her parents were the children of ministers, and her mother was strict about church attendance. Later asked if she had had a religious upbringing, Margaret answered, "And then some!"

Kenneth's father had been a minister in various Protestant denominations. He died before Margaret was born. Her grandfather on her mother's side lived until Margaret was fourteen. A Quaker pastor, he was like Kenneth in his attitude toward children; he never talked down to them. Young Margaret would sometimes sit on his lap as he was typing his sermons. He would read passages aloud, asking for her comments. His spiritual talks involved concepts like integrity, equality, and community, not to mention God. He knew that children rarely paid attention during church services, but he felt that Margaret was different, and he genuinely wanted to know her opinions. She responded enthusiastically, asking questions such as "What does 'integrity' mean?" and "Is it ever okay to lie?" He patiently answered, treating her with respect.

He was attentive in other ways. When they were listening to a baseball game on the radio, he would turn off the set if a beer ad came on, carefully counting the seconds until the ad was over. Then he would turn the radio back on, just as the game was resuming. Of course, Margaret was very curious about what she had missed.

Like many people with an inquisitive spirit, Margaret had a rebellious streak. Once, when she was around twelve, her parents went out of town for several days to attend a funeral. They left her in charge of her brother and sister, giving her a budget for food and other expenses. Seizing the opportunity, Margaret used some of the funds to stock up on the fixings for hot fudge sundaes, making whole meals of the treat so that for years afterward her siblings couldn't stand the sight of a hot fudge sundae.

• • •

Throughout Margaret's childhood, Kenneth's career in education evolved, from high school teacher, to principal, to school superintendent, to college professor, with his salary getting a small boost at each new stage. "My father didn't think of it as advancement," Margaret said later. "He needed to raise more money to buy more pairs of shoes and other necessities for the family." Meanwhile, her mother's career hardly changed, which was the way Esther liked it. Her specialty was teaching high school English and home economics—subjects she loved.

Home ec was a course required for every schoolgirl. The chief topics were cooking, sewing, and cleaning. Esther especially loved sewing, and she spent hours making most of the clothes for her family. This was common during the Depression and World War II. Home-cooked meals were also the norm, as was zealous house cleaning. These pursuits never appealed to Margaret, and home ec was the only school subject that she didn't like. She would have much preferred shop—the wood- and metal-working course that boys took.

"My mother used to get upset at me because I would spend all my time on my studies and not want to help around the house," Margaret remembered. "Of course, she wouldn't get upset at my brother for the same thing. My attitude was, 'I will do it if he does it. What's fair is fair!'"

"I didn't like to be treated in a way that I didn't think was fair, and I didn't like others to be treated that way either," she continued. "My father and grandfather instilled me with that. It never occurred to them that I was different because I was a girl. To them, I was just a person."

If Margaret and her mother didn't see eye to eye about chores, they both loved music. But here, too, they had their differences. Her mother was fond of classical music, which she played expertly on the piano. Margaret was more attracted to popular music, which she listened to

Margaret (center), around the time her family moved to Ripley, Michigan. She is flanked by her brothers, David and John, and her sister, Kathryn.

on the radio. As Margaret got older, her musical influences changed—from the inspiring hymns she sang in church, songs like "For the Beauty of the Earth" and "All Things Bright and Beautiful," to the even more stirring gospel tunes recorded by Mahalia Jackson, a Black singer living in Chicago. In the mid-1950s, Elvis Presley drew on both of these traditions, combined with African American blues and Appalachian country music, to create an exciting new sound that Margaret adored. It was rock and roll, and it horrified many grown-ups.

• • •

Margaret turned fifteen the summer of 1951, and the family made yet another move—to Ripley at the other end of the U.P., nearly three hundred miles from Sault Ste. Marie. In the heart of Michigan's Copper Country, Ripley was a small town near Kenneth's new posting at his college's main campus. That fall Margaret started her sophomore year of high school in Hancock, the town next to Ripley. Every morning the "Ripley girls"—about a dozen girls from all different grades—would assemble and walk the mile and a half to the Hancock public schools, and every afternoon they would make the trek back. The route passed along the Keweenaw Waterway, which had once carried giant ore haulers to and from the copper mines in the region. The mines were mostly closed now, but copper mining would play an important role in Margaret's education.

The principal at Hancock High was a woman named Sylvia Eskola, called "Old Lady Eskola" by the students. A severe taskmaster, she pushed them to excel and didn't tolerate misbehavior. One memorable regulation was that couples at school dances had to stay at least a foot away from their partners, which Principal Eskola enforced with a ruler. Margaret thrived, largely because she enjoyed her studies. She did particularly well in math, which pleased her teachers. This encouraged her to apply herself even harder. Thanks to her father, she also did well in literature and writing. But her mediocre performance in home ec eventually cost her the honor of being high school valedictorian. She came in second behind a girl who had straight As, including in home ec.

Margaret also thrived on the social scene. In her junior year she was voted homecoming queen, and the students at her father's college elected her snow queen at their winter festival. She was even asked to enter the Miss Michigan pageant—the preliminary to the Miss America competition. However, that was too much for Kenneth. He was open-minded about many things, but here "he was old-fashioned," Margaret reflected.

Fortunately, there were other adventures in Ripley.

Railcar carrying copper ore from a mine overlooking Hancock, Michigan, late 1800s. On the opposite bank is Houghton, site of the main campus of the Michigan College of Mining and Technology.

In Keweenawland
MICHIGAN'S UPPER PENINSULA
VISIT A COPPER MINE

Promotional brochure for the Arcadian Copper Mine.

AN EXCITING ADVENTURE!

Make an actual underground trip into
real copper mine! See geological won-
ure created eons ago; see awe
rkings deep inside
exciting

CHAPTER 3

THE BANANA MINE

AS TEENAGERS, MARGARET AND MANY OF HER friends joined the working world. Holding a part-time or summer job was a rite of passage for young people, giving them a new sense of freedom and responsibility. And, of course, they were paid—even if they earned less than the federal minimum wage at the time, which was seventy-five cents an hour and did not apply to most of the jobs that teenagers could get.

Margaret's first job was at the Woolworth store in Sault Ste Marie. Woolworth was a national chain of five-and-dimes, where merchandise generally cost a nickel or a dime. Most Woolworths also had a lunch counter where patrons could get hot meals, ice cream, and sodas. At the time, Margaret was younger than the minimum age for such work, which was fourteen. However, the law was not strictly enforced.

From the beginning, her plan was to save for college and personal expenses—for example, new ice skates. When she moved to Ripley, she took waitressing jobs at restaurants in the area: Joe's Chicken Basket and the Isle Royale Dining Room. Waitressing occupied her evenings. For daytime summer employment, she signed on at a nearby business: the Arcadian Copper Mine, where tourists could get an "unforgettable vacation experience!" according to the promotional brochure.

Arvo Walitalo (far left) at the entrance to his tourist mine.

• • •

Shut down decades earlier, the Arcadian Mine had for a time been used for storing bananas, since the temperature inside was a constant 42 degrees Fahrenheit, making it like a giant refrigerator. People took to calling it the "banana mine." Then in 1950, a local half-Finnish, half–American Indian entrepreneur named Arvo Walitalo leased part of it for practically nothing with two partners and reopened one tunnel as a tourist attraction.

GREETINGS FROM THE *Michigan* **COPPER** *Country*

CHUNK OF COPPER — 18000 POUNDS

Copper production reached a peak in Michigan in the 1910s. By Margaret's time in the 1950s, many mines had closed.

A former well digger with a gift for promotion, Arvo insisted, "Our mine is real! No tinsel, no flim-flam, no sucker bait," meaning he had no intention of cheating customers with a fake experience. He promised that visitors would "play the game of mining and come out with an education."

To provide that education, Arvo hired Margaret as his first guide. He asked her to learn all she could about the life of miners and how they extracted copper. Before each tour, she donned a hard hat and a miner's jacket, and made sure visitors did the same. Then this petite high schooler, wearing bobby socks and jeans, led the curious group through a big door in the hillside, beneath a sign that said, "Arcadian Copper Mine No. 9." It was the ninth passageway into a network of tunnels and shafts where hundreds of miners had toiled in the early 1900s.

The experience was cold, clammy, slightly scary, and also thrilling.

As she led sightseers deeper and deeper into the labyrinth, Margaret explained how copper in the region was in an unusually pure state, which Indians had long ago discovered. In other copper mines around the world, the metal was bound with different minerals, and the ore had to be crushed and processed to extract the copper. But geological forces in the Upper Peninsula had left chunks of pure copper embedded in the surrounding rock, ready for easy recovery. Often silver, amethyst, quartz, and other sparkling minerals were also present. Although mining operations had long since ceased, flecks of copper still glittered in the tunnel walls.

In the beginning, only one or two families a day made the trek to Ripley's out-of-the-way tourist attraction. But Arvo was such an

Tourists learn how copper ore was extracted and transported out of the Arcadian Mine.

effective promoter and Margaret such an enthusiastic teacher that soon hundreds of people a day were visiting the Arcadian Mine. Margaret had to hire and train other guides, and she made her brother David her chief assistant. She also convinced Arvo to open a gift shop, where she served as manager, selling postcards, copper jewelry, and other souvenirs. And since Arvo had only a fourth-grade education, she also handled the bookkeeping. No one had job titles, but teenage Margaret essentially became the chief executive officer, running the business and advising Arvo on all sorts of improvements. One piece of advice he didn't take was her ardent desire that he open a Dairy Queen at the site. The pioneer of soft-serve ice cream, Dairy Queen was a favorite with Margaret and her friends. Unfortunately, Arvo never followed up on this excellent suggestion.

• • •

His reluctance to branch out into soft-serve ice cream might have been because his mine was paying off "like a slot machine on a binge," as a reporter later put it. Arvo had enough income to buy three Cadillacs, and he spent the off-season traveling to tourist spots around North America to learn new tricks of the trade. One simple strategy: He would slap free bumper-sticker ads for the mine on visitors' cars.

Margaret was proud of the mine's success, and it didn't occur to her to ask for a raise until all her guides, including her brother, threatened to go on strike. She approached her boss: "Arvo, they're all going to quit unless you give them a raise. And by the way, I make what they do, so can I have a raise too?" He agreed to a small increase for everybody.

Margaret's biggest benefit by far was job satisfaction. "I was everywhere," she fondly mused. "If Arvo couldn't do it, I did it. It was like I owned the place." She worked at the mine every summer through high school and even afterward. "You could say I went to management school in the Arcadian Copper Mine. That's where I learned how to manage people and solve problems as they came up."

Margaret once discovered a huge chunk of native copper embedded in a tunnel wall. Arvo had told her she could keep any copper pieces she found in the mine, so she extracted it, lifted it into a tram car on rails, and wheeled it out. Excited, she showed it to Arvo.

"Oh, no, no, no. I'm keeping that," he insisted.

"But you promised!" Margaret objected. "That's not fair!"

"Let me think about it," he said. The next day he came back with the sample cut neatly in half. They split it as partners.

An eight-ton mass of pure copper mined on the Upper Peninsula. Margaret's "huge chunk" was considerably smaller.

Margaret could easily have stayed, which was the typical career path at the time. Young people would finish high school (or, in Arvo's case, fourth grade), find a job, eventually get married, and settle down, usually in their hometowns or not far away. But America was changing in the aftermath of World War II. The economy was thriving, and there was a huge demand for high-technology workers. The mine had stimulated Margaret's interest in geology, and she might have pursued that with a focus on copper mining. But she was less interested in science and technology than in the mathematics that made these fields so powerful. Math was the universal language of practically all technical subjects. She found it fun, and her goal was to teach this vital and fascinating discipline.

But to do that, she had to go to college first.

Angell Hall, the focal point for thousands of students at the University of Michigan, Ann Arbor.

CHAPTER 4

COLLEGE WOMAN

"I DON'T WANT TO GO TO COLLEGE!" MARGARET blurted out one day in a fit of rebellion.

"That's okay," said her father. He knew she would change her mind, but he wanted her to feel in control of her tumultuous teenage life.

Margaret had no intention of staying in Ripley. On the other hand, she didn't like the idea that she was on a regimented path to adulthood either, with college and a lifetime of teaching ahead of her. Furthermore, leaving home was such a major change that she just wished time would stop so she could catch her breath and consider her options. The way she saw it, there were four possibilities.

Option 1: Keep working for Arvo. Arvo Walitalo knew how much Margaret contributed to his business. Given her low salary, she was a bargain, and he was eager to keep her as long as she wanted to stick around. It never occurred to him that he could make it worth her while by doubling her salary or sharing the profits that were mounting from her astute management.

Option 2: Get married. A pretty homecoming queen like Margaret would have no trouble attracting suitors. In that era of stay-at-home mothers, she could have married a promising young man, kept house, and raised their growing brood of children as he advanced in his job. This was not an inviting prospect to someone who wanted her own career and who hated home ec.

Option 3: Strike out on her own. In the 1950s, a high school diploma qualified a woman for an entry-level position in an office, bank, store, or other business. Especially adventurous young women would move to a big city, find female roommates, land a job, and experience the thrill of independence. For Margaret, such freedom and self-sufficiency had their attractions.

Option 4: Go to college. Margaret had always pictured herself as a teacher, and this required a college degree. Both of her parents were teachers, and they had instilled in her a love of learning. Both of her grandfathers were ministers—which is a kind of teacher— and one of them had even run a school. Her grandmother on one side was a journalist, and her grandmother on the other side was a musician—both fields that benefit from higher education. Furthermore, Margaret excelled at school and really liked it. What other choice was there?

• • •

Once Margaret reached the obvious conclusion to go to college, she had to decide which one. Her grades were good enough for admission practically anywhere. Her mother and her mother's parents had gone to Earlham College in Indiana. Established by the Quakers, Earlham specialized in the liberal arts—literature, philosophy, languages, mathematics, science, and social sciences—rather than in professional subjects such as business and engineering.

Margaret's father had also gone to a liberal arts college, Olivet in Michigan. Like Earlham, Olivet had only a few hundred students. Having grown up in small towns, Margaret would have felt at home in either place. However, Kenneth had earned a master's degree in philosophy at the University of Michigan in Ann Arbor, which had thousands of students, studying every conceivable subject. The excitement of being around so many young people pursuing such diverse interests appealed to Margaret. She decided the large university was the place for her.

• • •

When Margaret arrived to register at Michigan in September 1954, the headline in the student newspaper read: "18,500 Enrollment Expected." That was nearly a hundred times more people than lived in Ripley! The Michigan campus was a sprawling and vibrant city of the young. Liberal arts students like Margaret attended classes in the center of campus. Law students mastered their profession in the adjoining quadrangle. On the periphery were the medical and dental schools. Architecture, engineering, business, and other disciplines resided in buildings clustered here and there. There were also libraries, auditoriums, museums, dorms, fraternities, and sororities—not to mention sports facilities surrounding the mammoth Michigan Stadium, which could hold more than ninety-seven thousand cheering football fans. Furthermore, the city of Ann Arbor itself had fifty thousand residents.

It was easy to get lost in the crowd at Michigan. The experience could be intimidating, but it also gave new students like Margaret a thrilling sense of freedom. On the other hand, female students, known as coeds, were held on a tight leash by the dean of women, Deborah

Bacon. She had been a combat nurse during World War II and was a bit like Old Lady Eskola from Hancock High. Dean Bacon enforced a strict curfew and a dress code (no shorts, no pedal pushers, no jeans). She banned kissing, famously telling the male students "to keep their hands off my women!" Parties had to be approved in advance and chaperoned. Drinking alcohol was prohibited. And in an era when smoking was widespread, women were allowed to light up only in certain areas.

Dean of Women's Ruling on Bermudas

ACCORDING TO a recent announcement by the Office of the Dean of Women, the University will start enforcing the ban on Bermuda shorts, pedal pushers, jeans and short shorts, on the books for quite some time now but largely ignored in the past.

"Violations will be dealt with firmly," quoth the Dean because, "Students should be dressed accordingly in this business center of an international university."

All seems to be part of a new and vicious trend. Christian Dior started it last spring when he shocked and frightened the world by announcing that henceforth efforts would be made to "straighten the line" by deemphasizing the bust. Now our University administrators are taking up the gauntlet and deemphasizing legs. What next?

There are two basic issues at stake and they must be treated with proper levity.

First, there is the problem of what constitutes dignity. A very pretty coed, attired in a pair of stunning plaid bermudas, questioned, "Must we wear skirts to look dignified?" In effect the new ruling answers "Yes." Perhaps, but the coed certainly struck us as being dignified.

The second and more serious problem is that

of governmental authority as contrasted with democratic freedoms. John Stuart Mill, who often wore shorts, pointed out in his classic doctrine, ON LIBERTY, that it is not the function of government (in this case the University) to impose the ethics of one sector of society unwillingly on another sector.

Since bermuda shorts are acceptable on most college campuses, indeed represent one of the most wide-spread clothing innovations in recent years, we may assume that the question of propriety involved is not of an ethical or moral nature, but rather a simple matter of opinion. If this is true, then it remains for each coed to decide for herself what constitutes dignity.

For some reason University administrators have always found it necessary to bury the student under an overwhelming number of regulations. We are one of the few schools that still maintain a driving ban, parties have to be registered, chaperoned and approved to be legal, drinking is illegal —in fact practically everything is illegal. And now, as if that wasn't enough, they're telling us what to wear. It looks bad, Mr. Mill.

—Gail Goldstein
Lee Marks

Two University of Michigan students argue against the dean of women's ban on Bermuda shorts.

Male students had greater freedom, but they were still subject to the dean of men. He spent his time policing their pranks, the most popular being "panty raids," which were mostly harmless mass break-ins at women's dorms.

Despite the temptation to run wild, Margaret was too busy to get into trouble. Worried that her education at a small-town high school put her at a disadvantage, she studied nonstop, focusing on her math courses. She was also taking religion and sociology. The religion class was her first formal introduction to ideas that she had often discussed with her father and grandfather. The course took a comparative approach, sending students to worship services at every kind of religious institution in the area. Students then had to evaluate the similarities and differences among all the ways that humans managed their spiritual lives. This appealed to her almost as much as math.

During final exams in December, Margaret realized with horror that she had been neglecting her sociology course, since her other work had led her to skip most of the required reading in the textbook. The night before the exam, with not enough time to catch up, she memorized the glossary at the back of the book. The next day the test had a single essay question, "What is man?" She wrote for an hour straight, using every term she had memorized. She got an A, and the impressed professor urged her to major in sociology.

Margaret got an A in everything else too. She had made the most promising start imaginable at Michigan. But she had decided that one semester at this crowded, cacophonous place was enough for her. She would transfer to the calm of Earlham in the new year.

Margaret is crowned
Homecoming Queen at
Earlham College, 1956.

CHAPTER 5

EARLHAM

QUIET IS A SPECIALTY OF THE QUAKERS, WHO incorporate silent meditation into their worship services. During these serene moments, you are encouraged to clear your mind and tune in to any spiritual messages that are within you. If you feel moved, you may stand and say that message aloud. Such a doctrine stimulates introspection, and Earlham's faculty and students tended to be unusually thoughtful.

Like Margaret, many students at Earlham came from Quaker backgrounds. But other faiths were represented as well, and the school's religious tradition provided "a unity of tone" rather than a required set of beliefs. Students were free to try out whatever ideas they liked, but always in the background were the moral principles and intellectual rigor and modesty of the Quakers. The college was small too, only eight hundred students, which was less than a twentieth the size of the University of Michigan. However, as one professor observed, "A mountain is far superior in size to a diamond, but it may not be size that really counts . . . There can be genuine merit in smallness."

Tree-lined paths in the heart of
Earlham College

• • •

Not only was Earlham a serious community where one could get a
good education, but according to Margaret's Aunt Maggie, it was "so
much fun!" Maggie was Margaret's mother's youngest sister, and she
had followed the family tradition of attending Earlham. Aware that
Margaret wanted to try something different from the gigantic university, she told her, "You really ought to go to Earlham."

So Margaret did, and Aunt Maggie was right. What made Earlham
fun was not frivolity but friendliness. Classes were typically small, professors were always accessible, and students lived, studied, and relaxed
together. Margaret flourished—and not just in her studies. She single-

handedly enhanced the cultural climate at Earlham by introducing the music of Elvis Presley, who was just emerging as a rock and roll star. Margaret had first heard him on the radio during her senior year at Hancock High. At Earlham, she would often do her homework in the student lounge where the jukebox had been loaded with records at her recommendation. She had no trouble doing math problems to the lyrics and beat of "That's All Right" or "Good Rockin' Tonight" or "Milkcow Blues Boogie." Having brought Elvis to this quiet Quaker community, Margaret earned a reputation as a rebel.

She was a rebel in other ways too. Her dorm had a strict evening curfew, which she broke more than any student before her. This was due to her preference for keeping late hours. One morning at 4:00 a.m., she held a clothes swap with other coeds. Margaret was known for her simple but lovely outfits, which were handmade by her mother. As is only natural, she took her wardrobe for granted and admired the store-bought clothes worn by her friends. So while most of the campus was asleep, she gave female students an opportunity to trade anything they wanted at an impromptu fashion show and barter session. As the Sun rose, everyone felt rich with their new acquisitions.

. . .

Perhaps "rebel" is too strong a word for Margaret. She was a non-conformist, true, but she was also unfailingly polite and considerate, which won her many friends. During a charity auction her freshman year, her offer to provide cleaning service for a full day (hardly her favorite activity) prompted a winning bid of $64 from one of the men's dorms, equal to about $700 in today's terms. The summer after her sophomore year, in addition to a shift at the Arcadian Mine, she worked as a volunteer, teaching children with disabilities how to swim. That fall, Margaret was elected Earlham's homecoming queen—the same honor she had won in high school. The yearbook's coverage of the event included a photo of her raking leaves for the campus cleanup, with the text: "She is known on campus for her friendly smile and winning personality."

The editors might have added that she was renowned for her cleverness too. For example, before Margaret graduated she had to pass a fitness test. One of the simple requirements was to perform a somersault. However, Margaret had a childhood aversion to somersaults that she couldn't conquer. Worried that this phobia might prevent her from graduating, she had to think outside the box. It occurred to her that the rule did not specify where the somersault took place. Since she was a good swimmer, she convinced the fitness

Students traditionally did the fall cleanup on the day before Homecoming. Here, the queen-to-be does her part.

judge to let her do it underwater, which was a snap for her. "If you can't solve it, put it in a different place," she later said, "and don't be afraid to disagree with the experts . . . Just because people say it's never going to work, that doesn't mean you have to give up."

No one would ever accuse Margaret of giving up.

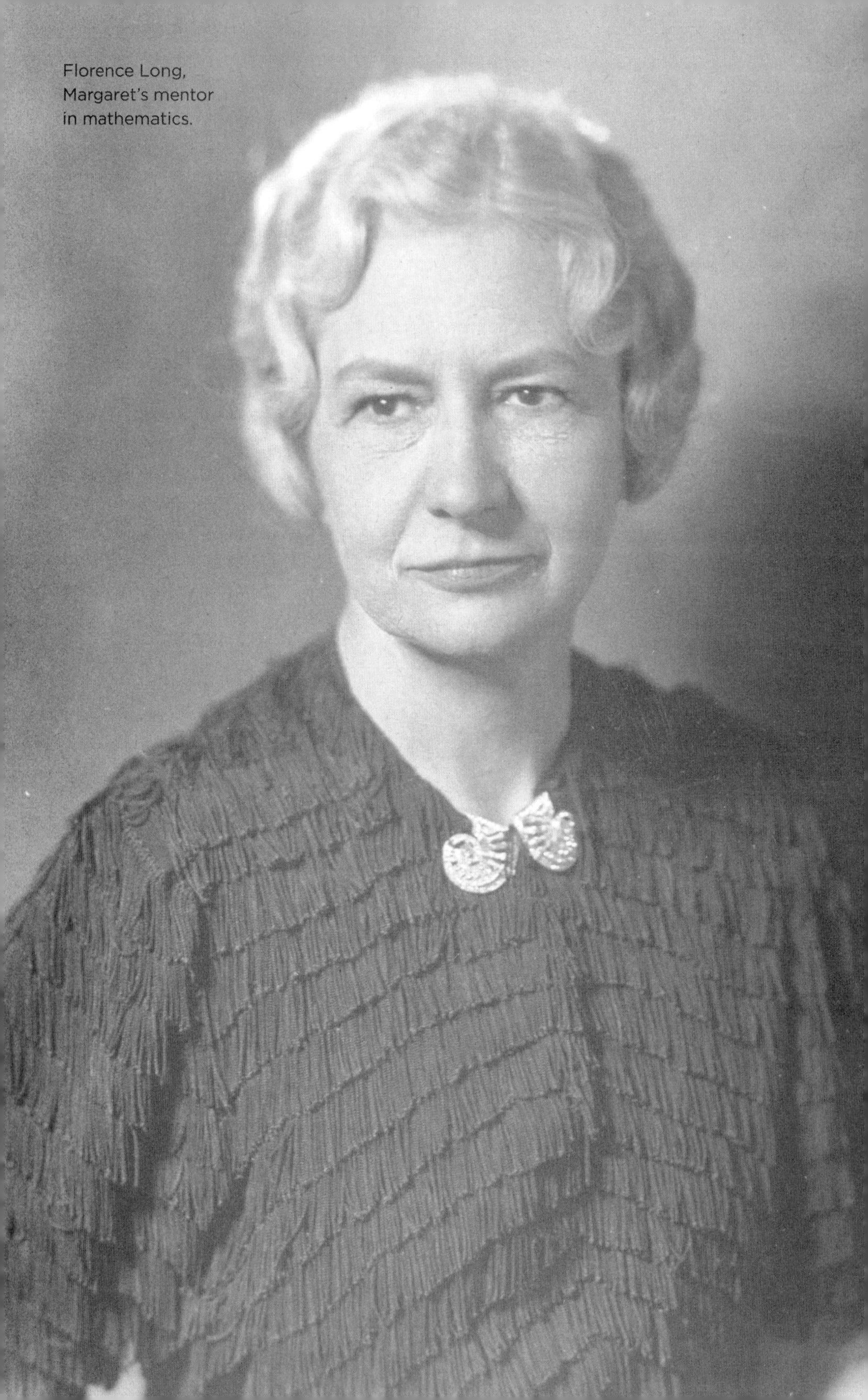
Florence Long, Margaret's mentor in mathematics.

CHAPTER 6
MATH, PHILOSOPHY, AND RELIGION

OF COURSE COLLEGE IS ABOUT EDUCATION, AND here Margaret was in luck. Earlham's senior math professor was a woman, Florence Long. She became Margaret's mentor and role model. Like Margaret, Professor Long came from a small town. She graduated from Earlham in 1913 and then did advanced work in mathematics at Bryn Mawr, a women's college in Pennsylvania. After that she returned to Earlham to teach math for the rest of her career. She never married. The rumor among students was that she had been engaged to a young man who was killed in World War I, in which over one hundred thousand American soldiers died. Heartbroken, she threw herself into teaching. During summer vacations, she liked to travel the world by train and ocean liner. But then in the fall she would return to Earlham and her students, who were like her children to her.

"Everybody looked up to her," Margaret observed. "She was just a very warm and brilliant human being. It wasn't what she said, it's just who she was. She would invite us to her house from time to time for cucumber sandwiches with mayonnaise. But when she'd get up and lecture, I thought, 'Oh, my God, I want to do what she's doing.'"

What Professor Long was doing was abstract mathematics—theorems and proofs—which is the bedrock of all mathematics. This contrasts with applied mathematics, which is the use of math to solve practical problems in engineering, science, economics, and other fields. True to Margaret's love of ideas, she preferred math in its abstract, pure form. One result was that she paid less attention than she should have to her statistics class, which was taught by another professor. A required course for math majors, statistics involves the analysis of data and is one of the most useful applications of math. Luckily, Margaret's good friend Jean Hiatt also majored in math and had excelled at statistics. The night before Margaret's final exam, Jean gave her a marathon cram session, which Margaret retained long enough to ace the test.

Margaret and Jean stood out as math majors among their female classmates, who mostly concentrated in elementary education, English, and psychology. Professor Long struggled against the reluctance of many women to pursue math. She subscribed to the credo of Charlotte Angas Scott, a British mathematician who headed the department at Bryn Mawr when Long was there. Scott insisted that women were just as capable of rigorous achievement in mathematics as men, and she made sure that her students performed at the highest level possible. "I am most disturbed and disappointed [by] the position that intellectual pursuits must be 'watered down' to make them suitable for women," Scott wrote, "and that a lower standard must be adopted at a woman's college than in a man's."

Margaret discovered that not everyone at Earlham was as open to female intellectual achievement as Professor Long. Her physics instructor—a man—believed that women did not belong in technical fields and discouraged coeds from taking his classes. Among the older generation of male teachers, there was an attitude that a woman "wasted her education by majoring in men's courses," by implication science and math. Margaret took introductory physics anyway and got an A.

· · ·

Margaret got more respect in her philosophy courses than in physics. People tend to think of philosophy as a subject about personal preferences, as in, "What is your philosophy of life?" But philosophy is just as rigorous as mathematics, which relies on a branch of philosophy called logic. Earlham was fortunate to have a first-rate faculty in the subject, headed by one of the nation's most prominent philosophers, Professor Elton Trueblood. Although Margaret didn't take any of his courses, Professor Trueblood set the tone for the department. Earlham students from many different majors flocked to his lectures on general philosophy, which covered a huge array of ideas starting with the principles of reasoned argument, an activity familiar to any mathematician. Professor Trueblood believed that students learned best when they debated issues with each other, reaching their own conclusions rather than relying on the teacher for the answers. If he thought his pupils were on the wrong track in a discussion, he would ask a probing question or propose a view opposite his own to test their convictions. The interchange was surprisingly fun.

A devout Quaker, Professor Trueblood also taught philosophy of religion using the same approach. No system of beliefs was taken for

Philosopher Elton Trueblood pauses for a discussion at a campus construction site.

granted, and students explored a wide range of religious and ethical concepts, debating their pros and cons. Even atheism was treated as an acceptable alternative—if a student supported it with sound arguments.

Margaret may have majored in math, but she took as many philosophy courses as she could. She did so well, especially in the philosophy of religion, that she got a very interesting offer during her senior year. Without her knowledge, at least one of her professors had recommended her to a theological seminary for graduate study. That institution checked her record and decided to offer her a paid fellowship—again without Margaret even applying. The grant was prestigious, and it was a career path to the ministry or a teaching job in religion.

Margaret didn't know what to do. The grant was a great honor that would have pleased her minister grandfathers. Plus it would be fun to delve into a subject that she found so fascinating. Yet doing it in homage to her late grandfathers or because it was intellectually interesting wasn't in the spirit of the offer. She felt she had to do it for the *right* reasons, and on reflection, she wasn't sure she believed in God. She wasn't sure she *didn't* believe in God either. She just didn't know.

She explained this when she declined the offer, worrying that her professors might be angry. But they understood. Her outlook wasn't atheism, they explained, but agnosticism, which is the view that God's existence cannot be established one way or the other. Professor Trueblood himself was sympathetic to this stance and had written: "No truly devout person can raise any objection to this position. Indeed, the agnostic mood . . . is far more fruitful than is the mood of rigid dogmatism"—the unreasoning adherence to a set of beliefs.

Still, most of her professors at Earlham *did* believe in God. Even so, they praised her for her honesty and thoughtfulness. One even told her, "God gave you the brains to think about things like this."

So mathematics it would be, and Margaret's fondest wish was to have a career teaching abstract math in college, just like Florence Long.

Earlham scholars.

CHARLOTTE ANGAS SCOTT

Margaret's mentor at Earlham, Florence Long, studied under one of the most esteemed mathematics educators of the day, Charlotte Angas Scott, at Bryn Mawr College in Pennsylvania. Raised in England, Scott came from a family much like Margaret's: Her father and grandfather were both ministers and teachers, and the family loved to tackle mathematical puzzles for entertainment. Due to a lack of educational opportunities for girls, Scott was tutored at home until she was ready for Girton College, one of Britain's first residential colleges for women, which was associated with the then all-male University of Cambridge. At the time, Girton had no courses in mathematics, so Scott attended lectures at Cambridge, where the two sexes were treated very differently. Women had to have chaperones and were required to enter and leave class apart from the men. One woman

Mathematician Charlotte Angas Scott.

described having to sit with female students in the back of a lecture hall behind a screen so as not to distract the male scholars. Obviously, this would make it difficult to see math equations on the chalkboard.

Despite these obstacles, Scott excelled, eventually earning the first doctorate in mathematics ever awarded to a woman in Britain. In 1885, she sailed to the United States to head the math department at the brand-new women's college, Bryn Mawr. In her forty-year career at Bryn Mawr, she trained some of America's most prominent female mathematicians, directing their research on famous unsolved problems and other topics in abstract mathematics.

In 1925, Scott retired to England, where she lived like a character in a British mystery, tending her garden and using her mathematical expertise to wager on horse races, placing bets through her doctor's bookie. According to her doctor, she didn't do too badly.

BRYN MAWR COLLEGE.

EXAMINATION FOR MATRICULATION.

GROUP I. (*Counted as two sections.*)

ALGEBRA.
THREE HOURS.

PART I.
(*Counted as one section.*)

1. Prove that
$$\frac{1 + 2\sqrt{3} + \sqrt{5}}{\sqrt{3} + 1} = 4.904 \ldots$$

2. What are the meanings of the symbols $x^{-\frac{1}{2}}$, x°? Simplify
$$\frac{\{(x^2)^{m-n}\}^{m+n} \times (x^3)^{\frac{2n^2}{3} - m^2}}{\left(\frac{1}{x}\right)^m \times x^{m(m+1)}}.$$

Page 1 of a math exam given to Bryn Mawr applicants during Scott's tenure on the faculty.

IS THIS TOMORROW

AMERICA UNDER COMMUNISM

Cover of a 1947 comic book warning against the communist menace.

CHAPTER 7

THE COLD WARRIOR

ANOTHER OF EARLHAM'S NOTABLE TEACHERS WAS E. Merrill Root, a poet and professor of English. Again, Margaret didn't take his courses, but his controversial ideas were discussed all over campus. In the classroom, Professor Root taught his students to be sensitive and effective writers, and he introduced them to the joys of great literature. Outside of class, he was a political firebrand, obsessed with the menace posed by the Soviet Union and its communist system.

Like many poets and intellectuals, Root had been enthusiastic about the Russian Communist Revolution in 1917, which led to the creation of the Soviet Union (officially the Union of Soviet Socialist Republics). The new nation was the world's first communist state, seizing land, factories, and other property for the public good and promising economic security and freedom for all its citizens. But as the brutality of the Soviet regime became clear in the 1930s and 1940s, Root and many others changed their minds. Anticommunism became especially strong in America during the Cold War, which was the period of political tension between the Soviet Union and the United States that followed the end of World War II in 1945 and lasted nearly half a century. The Cold War was at its height when Margaret was at Earlham.

• • •

Professor Root was careful not to discuss politics in his English classes, but the whole campus—indeed the whole country—knew his radical views, since he wrote opinion pieces in national periodicals and published two books, all sounding the alarm in the most uncompromising way. "Communists talk abstractly of 'liquidating' their 'class enemies,'" he wrote, "which sounds as harmless as pouring cyanide on the pages of a telephone directory. But the poet or the plain man sees the concrete reality: he sees the pistol placed behind the right ear; he hears the muffled bang."

In this poster from 1920, Russian communists prepare to liquidate a Western enemy in the distance.

This Soviet stamp celebrates Sputnik, "the world's first man-made satellite," launched by the Soviet Union on October 4, 1957.

Many Earlham faculty and alumni thought Root took things too far and urged his dismissal. But the president of the college, who also thought Root went too far, counseled tolerance. The zealous professor was "one of the most beloved and effective teachers on the Earlham staff," the president wrote to a critic. "We agree with his right to speak, as we agree that persons who hold another point of view have a similar right to speak."

Whether you agreed with Professor Root's opinions or not, the Soviet challenge to America was a cause for concern and a topic of discussion at Earlham and around the nation.

At the time, few Americans had traveled to the Soviet Union, and even fewer Soviets had come to the United States. As a result, it was hard to know what the conditions there were. The Soviet government boasted of its preeminence in a wide range of fields—military, medical, technological, cultural. But these claims were hard to judge.

That is, until the Soviets shocked the world by launching the world's first artificial satellite in October 1957, just after Margaret started her senior year. Called Sputnik, the satellite was humanity's

Elvis Presley in performance, 1956.

first step beyond the planet, and the Soviets—not the Americans—had done it.

"The United States is losing the cold war," Professor Root lamented. He traced the problem to his own profession, arguing that many college professors held communist beliefs, which they passed on to their students. In his view, this ideological influence undermined the country's traditional strengths of initiative, independence, and patriotism. He saw subversion elsewhere too. In a talk to students, he urged them "to retain those good qualities from the past which represent constant values—values that do not change with the time." He noted that Shakespeare, Beethoven, and the writer Ralph Waldo Emerson represented civilized values. These he contrasted with popular figures representing reprehensible values, among them a new recording star who was all the rage on campus—Elvis Presley.

Margaret and Jim at
Earlham, 1957–1958.

CHAPTER 8

JIM

JIM HAMILTON STOOD UP FOR ELVIS. HE WAS editor-in-chief of Earlham's student newspaper when Professor Root gave his talk attacking some of the cultural icons of the younger generation, including the soulful, gyrating singer.

In an eight-hundred-word editorial, Hamilton's paper politely criticized Professor Root for not being more open to change. "Root attempts to preserve the worthwhile values of the past—and this is good," the unsigned editorial commented. "But we must do more than merely keep the good from the past; we must *transcend* it." The editorial didn't actually say that Elvis transcended Beethoven, but it tried to put youth's craze for novelty in perspective. "Having reached a goal it is not enough merely to maintain it: we must search for new goals, for new truth, and a new type of perfection—in short a new way for civilization to grow."

Elvis probably never thought of it that way.

• • •

James Cox Hamilton was a year behind Margaret. He came from Meadville, Pennsylvania, where his grandfather ran the Keystone View

Company. Keystone was a world leader in stereographic images, which allowed people to experience faraway places through the magic of stereo photography, a technique that creates the sensation of three dimensions in a pair of still pictures. Originally marketed for home entertainment, stereo viewers spread to classrooms around the country, where they added a valuable visual component to lessons in geography, history, and the sciences. Some of the images even featured Jim and his sister, who posed in several scenes commissioned by the firm.

Jim's family ran a company that published stereo photographs for education and entertainment. This example shows the majestic Brooklyn Bridge.

Regardless of the company's success, Jim had little interest in going to work at Keystone. His passions were politics and debating—and also chemistry, which was his major at Earlham. As editor of the paper, he launched a campaign to analyze the effectiveness of Earlham's education, not just in academics but in moral matters as well. He also published pieces opposing some of the college's rules. For example, one editorial argued that students should have greater freedom to smoke on campus. At the time, about half of all American adults smoked, and Jim clearly believed it was demeaning for the college to restrict students to unpleasant smoking rooms. His view was that Earlham students should be treated as adults. He apparently didn't consider the health effects of smoking, nor did very many other people since the link between cigarettes and lung cancer was not yet clear.

Jim also encouraged fellow students to think more. Despite Earlham's reputation for academic excellence, many students didn't practice their mental skills outside of class. "Do people ever date to pick up a few new ideas from a person who is interesting?" one of his paper's editorials inquired. "This is not to say that socializing should not be fun," it went on. "However, when thinking is not only unimportant, but often ridiculed, we are building a weak foundation for later life, especially marriage. And we are limiting any intellectual growth we get here to the classroom, which is inadequate space for it."

Jim was editor in chief of Earlham's student newspaper, which criticized the more frivolous side of college life.

· · ·

One person who shared Jim's passion for ideas was Margaret. Both were serious about their studies, eager to learn new things, public spirited, and conscientious. Plus, they had a kindred sense of humor. In other words, they hit it off. By Margaret's senior year they were engaged to be married.

· · ·

Engaged college students were not at all unusual. Earlham even had housing units for married couples. Philosophy professor Elton Trueblood had written approvingly about this phenomenon: "The fact that the ordinary residential college, with both male and female students, leads normally to marriage between fellow students is neither an occasion for humor nor a defect, but a decided asset." He explained that coeducational colleges gathered young people with similar interests and then mixed them together in classes and extracurricular activities for several years, so it was little wonder that like minds inevitably found each other—as Margaret and Jim did.

They were married in a Quaker ceremony on campus in July 1958, a month after Margaret graduated. Margaret Heafield was now officially Margaret Heafield Hamilton. Since Jim needed another year to finish, they moved into married student housing, and Margaret went to work.

Her job interview took place in the local hospital while she was recovering from double pneumonia, possibly brought on by exhaustion during the last weeks of her senior year. The school system in the nearby small town of Boston, Indiana, needed a high school math and French teacher. They must have been desperate because they intruded on a seriously ill patient. "Yes," Margaret said feverishly, of course she could teach math. But French? She had only studied it for a year. "No problem," the school official replied. "You'll know more than the students."

One thing she didn't know was how to handle a classroom full of teenagers. Here, her friend Jean, who had graduated the year before and had started her own teaching career, came to the rescue. "Don't let the students push you around," Jean counseled. "If you do, you will lose control and never get it back." Margaret followed this advice, cultivating a take-charge manner. Combined with her management expertise developed at Arvo's mine, she was learning how to lead.

. . .

And so in the first year of their married life, Jim attended school and also worked part-time as a chemist's assistant, and Margaret taught math and French (listening to French tapes every day before class to stay ahead of her students). After Jim graduated, they both intended to go to graduate school: Margaret in mathematics and Jim in chemistry.

At least, that was the plan.

Spencer TRACY · Katharine HEPBURN

make the office such a wonderful place to love in!

A balky electronic computer sparks a love match in Hollywood's 1957 romantic comedy *Desk Set*.

—AND INTRODUCE YOU TO THE—

Desk Set

CINEMASCOPE
COLOR by DE LUXE   20th CENTURY-FOX

STARRING
GIG YOUNG · JOAN BLONDELL

PRODUCED BY
HENRY EPHRON

DIRECTED BY
WALTER LANG

SCREENPLAY BY
PHOEBE and HENRY EPHRON

BASED ON THE PLAY PRODUCED BY
ROBERT FRYER and LAWRENCE CARR
AND WRITTEN BY WILLIAM MARCHANT

CHAPTER 9

THINKING MACHINES

WHEN MARGARET WAS AT EARLHAM, SHE KNEW all about computers. In fact, she briefly *was* a computer. For centuries, the term had meant "a person who computes"—that is, someone who performs mathematical calculations, especially as a job. During one summer vacation Margaret worked as a human computer at the Travelers Insurance Company in Hartford, Connecticut. The firm was teaching her all about insurance with the goal of attracting her to the profession, which involves analyzing risk using mathematics. In return for this education, Margaret spent part of her time working in a room full of computers—all women—who were processing insurance data.

All day long, they calculated premiums and losses for an endless stream of cases. Each woman had a desktop mechanical calculator. Inside the machine were hundreds of wheels, levers, and springs, ingeniously organized to add, subtract, multiply, and divide. The human computers punched in numbers and hit operation keys. The calculators responded with staccato clicks and explosive clatters. Managers didn't have to worry about idle conversation in the room; the noise was deafening.

Women computers in the 1950s.

One day during a break, Margaret heard the women talking about a news article that predicted they would soon lose their jobs to an electronic computer, a mammoth machine that could do the work of the entire room—and more—with only a technician or two to mind it. Hollywood had even made a romantic comedy about the threat posed by these "thinking machines." *Desk Set* starred the classic acting duo Katharine Hepburn and Spencer Tracy. In the film, Tracy plays the inventor of an electronic brain that takes over a host of tasks at a television network, including fact research in the all-female reference library, headed by Hepburn's character. The computer engineer and the librarian argue over the value of a mindless thinking machine versus resourceful, if slower, humans. In typical Hollywood style, romance blossoms between the two stars, while the room-sized computer, with flashing lights and spinning tapes, makes outrageous mistakes and has a spectacular breakdown. Love triumphs, and modern technology is put in its place.

Desk Set was fiction, but electronic computers were indeed the wave of the future. And so was computer error, due to the difficulty of catching every fault in a complex computer program. True to the rumors at Travelers, the women Margaret had worked with were eventually moved to other tasks or laid off. Step by step, the world was beginning to realize that computers were no longer humans. They were a new kind of powerful but far-from-perfect machine.

Anyway, Margaret didn't think insurance was the career for her. She did very well in the summer program, and Travelers even offered to pay for her further studies. But she found insurance mathematics to be uninspiring. After all, it was mostly based on statistics, her least favorite math course at Earlham.

· · ·

Jim graduated from Earlham in June 1959. Both he and Margaret had applied and been accepted to graduate programs at Brandeis University in Waltham, Massachusetts. Furthermore, Margaret was due to have a baby that fall. During their drive east, they discussed how to handle these new commitments. Since they needed an income, one of them would have to work while the other attended school. They figured they would manage the new baby somehow. With the limitless confidence of a young couple, they decided that Jim would take the first turn in graduate school, while Margaret took a job—and had the baby. After Jim finished, they would switch roles. These deliberations were interrupted when their car broke down while on the road. Thanks to an emergency $200 loan from Margaret's father, they replaced it with another secondhand car and continued east toward their exciting new life.

In September, Jim started his chemistry program at Brandeis. Then two weeks before Thanksgiving, their daughter, Lauren, was born at a hospital in nearby Boston. In those days, women usually left the workforce, often permanently, after childbirth. But Margaret and Jim had no intention of doing things the usual way. They took turns with Lauren, aided by a babysitter, which allowed Margaret to go back to work after only a short break.

Her new job was writing software for a meteorology professor. In her quiet but assertive way, she was rebelling on two fronts: by pursuing the brand-new field of computer programming and doing it as a

Margaret, Lauren, and Jim, 1960.

young mother. Later in her career, she would be reproached by one of her male colleagues who didn't like the idea of working mothers. "You do what's right for you, and I'll do what's right for me," Margaret told him. He thought about it and decided he needed to be more open-minded. In time, they became good friends.

When Margaret accepted the software job, most people had no idea what a computer programmer did, much less what software was. Computers were considered so magical and mysterious that the mere act of building them seemed sufficient. Then you just turned them on, and they solved your problems. In a sense, that was true with the earliest electronic computers since their instructions for solving problems—their programs—were entirely wired in and could only be altered by laboriously rewiring the machine. That changed with stored-program computers, which had the flexibility to solve a wide range of problems by changing the instructions in the computer's memory. This was done by writing a new program in a special computer language, encoding it on a paper tape or a set of cards, then feeding the code into the computer. The job was so new that a new term had been invented to describe the instructions that a programmer writes: software.

In 1958, the year that Margaret graduated from Earlham, a well-known mathematician named John W. Tukey published a paper where he introduced the term "software" for the first time in print. Tukey was contrasting the "hardware" of physical computers (wires, circuits, data storage drives, and other parts) with intangible "software"—the sequence of steps that a machine must follow to solve a particular problem. Tukey himself saw the field as limited. "A few students and users will develop slowly into designers and programmers," he predicted, "but their number will be few." Like practically everyone else, he greatly underestimated the need for programmers and the challenges they faced.

Fresh from teaching high school, Margaret was now part of the growing software revolution. Succeeding at it would take the computational skills of a mathematician, the logical powers of a philosopher, and the patience of a new mother. It would also help to have the adventurous spirit of an explorer—and to be a bit of a rebel.

THE ENIAC WOMEN

When Margaret started out in computer programming, the field was dominated almost entirely by men. The situation looked very different two decades earlier, in the 1940s, mainly because software didn't yet exist. One of the innovative computers from that era was ENIAC, which stood for Electronic Numerical Integrator and Computer.

Programming ENIAC the old-fashioned way—by hand. Jean Jennings Bartik is crouching. Her colleague is Marlyn Wescoff Meltzer.

ENIAC was designed to calculate artillery firing tables for the U.S. Army during World War II. Mathematically adept young women were recruited to operate the machine, which involved physically rearranging cables and switches for every new set of equations. Around the lab the staff called this process "programming"—probably the first use of that word in connection with computers.

Setting ENIAC's main controls. Bartik stands at the left. On the right is Frances Bilas Spence.

"The assumption was that only women would do this," commented Jean Jennings Bartik, one of the original ENIAC women. "They considered programming a mundane, dull job—repetitive, where what you do is go out and you set switches and do things like that."

She added sarcastically: "And yes, of course, women are good at this, right?"

But Bartik and her colleagues took immense pride in their work, which called for detailed knowledge of ENIAC's circuitry and the ability to devise clever uses of the machine's limited operations to perform complicated calculations. "If the ENIAC's administrators had known how crucial programming would be to the functioning of the electronic computer and how complex it would prove to be," said Bartik, "they might have been more hesitant to give such an important role to women."

With Margaret's programming help, Edward Lorenz discovered that unexpected order emerges when a weather model is run repeatedly. The atmosphere behaves chaotically, but within distinct limits. In this graph, the outcome is a butterfly-like shape known as a Lorenz attractor.

CHAPTER 10

THE WEATHER
MAN

IN *DESK SET*, SPENCER TRACY'S CHARACTER IS A
computer engineer from the Massachusetts Institute of Technology.
The writers likely chose MIT because of its recent fame for creating
the Whirlwind computer, the fastest of its day and the first to respond
almost instantly to an operator's instructions. MIT was renowned in
other fields too, including meteorology.

In the summer of 1959, an MIT meteorology professor named
Edward Lorenz was searching for a research assistant who could help
him with computer programming. A colleague at Brandeis University
a few miles away suggested Margaret, newly arrived from Indiana with
her husband and looking for work. Lorenz had trained as a mathematician and recognized Margaret as someone who could understand the
equations of weather forecasting and figure out how to translate them
into computer code, even though she had never done it before. So he
hired her. "I was learning the computer at the same time he was," she
commented in hindsight. "It was an adventure!"

Lorenz was one of the few scientists anywhere who had his own
computer. In those days the U.S. Army, an insurance company, or a

university physics department might have a computer, but hardly any individuals did. Computers were just too big, expensive, and difficult to operate. But then the Royal McBee Corporation began selling a more compact computer that was about the size of a large desk. It cost around $50,000 (about half a million dollars today), and it was called the LGP-30. "He loved that computer," Margaret reminisced. "And he made me feel the same way about it."

The LGP-30, one of the world's first "personal" computers. The computing unit is the console to the right of the keyboard/printer. At the left is the input/output device, which employs perforated tape.

• • •

In the 1950s, weather forecasters studied historical weather patterns to learn how different weather systems develop. They used this knowledge to predict how today's conditions would evolve, guessing that specific conditions that turned out one way in the past would do the same in the future. Experienced forecasters could make accurate predictions for two, three, or even four days, but rarely beyond that. However, Lorenz and others were working on a technique that could produce much longer-range forecasts. Called the numerical method, it compiled data on the current temperature, pressure, air density, humidity, and wind direction, and then plugged these numbers into a set of equations designed to mimic the way the atmosphere behaves. The difference was between projecting what the weather would do based on the historical record and calculating it using precise measurements. Unfortunately, the equations were so complicated that solving them took longer than it did for the weather to actually happen! One expert estimated that sixty-four thousand people operating hand slide rules (see "The Other Onboard Computer," page 186) and calculating machines would be needed to staff a world weather forecasting center that could make timely predictions.

That's where electronic computers proved their worth. Together, Lorenz, his graduate students, and Margaret—far fewer than sixty-four thousand people—tried their hand at predicting global weather with the aid of the LGP-30. Professor Lorenz wrote the equations, and Margaret converted them to computer code. Then the LGP-30 sprang into action, simulating one day's worth of weather every minute—or about two years of weather during an overnight run of twelve hours. Lorenz wasn't yet producing usable forecasts, but he was laying the foundation for a deeper understanding of the weather—work that would lead him to a startling discovery.

• • •

Margaret liked to write code on the roof of the old army barracks where Lorenz had his offices. She mastered the operator's manual for the LGP-30 and learned its programming language. But translating the professor's equations was far from straightforward. She had to rethink everything she knew about mathematics. For example, in order to add two numbers, x and y, the LGP-30 required a program like this:

LOCATION	INSTRUCTIONS	COMMENTS
0100	b3750	Bring x to the accumulator
0101	a3751	Add y
0102	h0104	Store sum
0103	z0000	Stop
0104		Sum

In the middle column, a single letter is followed by the location in the computer's memory for the data or task. The letter b means "bring from memory"; a stands for "add"; h indicates "hold and store"; and z is "stop." In this example, numbers stored at locations 3750 and 3751 (track 37, locations 50 and 51) are added, and the answer ends up at location 0104, ready to be plugged into a new equation.

This program shows how the programmer tells the computer what to do. But like all digital computers, the LGP-30 converted instructions into binary code—a sequence of ones and zeroes corresponding to the presence or absence of magnetic charges in the computer's memory. As far as the LGP-30 was concerned, the first four lines of the middle column looked like this:

```
0000000000000001001001011100100
0000000000001110001001011100110
0000000000001100000000010001000
0000000000000000000000000000000
```

Margaret got so good at programming that not only could she instruct the computer in the complex equations of weather forecasting, but she could also read the ones and zeroes on the perforated output tape to find errors: ones that should be zeroes or vice versa. These she would correct by covering errant holes with Scotch tape or punching new holes with a sharp pencil, as needed. This quick fix was her own invention, and everyone loved it. "I would walk down the long hall in the meteorology department," she noted, "and people would stop to see how many holes I had taped or punched. They thought this was fascinating."

• • •

Meanwhile, Lorenz was wrestling with his equations, trying to get a set of mathematical terms and constants that acted like the weather.

An old expression goes, "as changeable as the weather." Lorenz wanted his equations to produce results that were just as changeable but not completely random. Weather is not random because it has large-scale, repeating patterns, such as hot summers and cold winters, or dry and wet seasons. Within these bounds, there can be enormous variability. That variability is what Lorenz wanted to predict.

Margaret would code and then run every new version of his equations, going out for lunch or leaving for the day until the computer finished its calculations. Lorenz would check the results and adjust his math. Then Margaret would run a new simulation. On some runs, everyone in the office would gather around the computer printer and watch the evolving weather systems.

One time Lorenz decided to stop the simulation and repeat part of it so he could focus on a particular detail. He backtracked and copied the numbers at the point where he wanted to restart and instructed the computer to take it from there. Then he left for a cup of coffee.

Lorenz studies a computer-generated weather model like those produced by Margaret's programs.

When he returned an hour later, expecting to see the same unfolding sequence of weather as before, he was astonished to find it was radically different.

"There must be some mistake," he thought. But in comparing the old run with the new one, he saw that everything matched perfectly at first. Then over time the two simulations diverged until they were wildly different. Searching for a cause, all Lorenz could find was that he had rounded off the starting set of numbers for the second run, deleting a few extra decimal places so the numbers varied by less than one part in a thousand, which was a trivial discrepancy that should have made no difference. But it did. It made a *huge* difference.

Lorenz had discovered the "butterfly effect," also known as sensitive dependence on initial conditions. The butterfly analogy may come from Lorenz's later paper, "Predictability: Does the Flap of a Butterfly's Wings in Brazil Set Off a Tornado in Texas?" The surprising answer is, in theory it could.

• • •

Lorenz's pioneer report alluding to the butterfly effect credited only one other person: "The writer is greatly indebted to Mrs. Margaret Hamilton for her assistance in performing the many numerical computations which were necessary in this work." At the time, it was very unusual to acknowledge a research assistant on a scientific paper. But Lorenz was giving credit where credit was due.

Margaret was the ideal assistant, and he suggested that she become a scientist in his field. Of course, her sociology professor at the University of Michigan, her religion professors at Earlham, and the Travelers Insurance Company had all made the same suggestion:

They wanted her to join *their* professions. Margaret's practice was to get deeply involved in whatever she was doing and do the best job she possibly could. This simple habit made her a coveted colleague. She was already attending Lorenz's lectures, and he strongly urged her to enter graduate school in meteorology. Although she was fascinated by weather forecasting, she had to keep her eye on the ball. Her responsibility at that moment was to earn money and care for Lauren while Jim was in graduate school. When he finished, *then* she could go to graduate school. Her plan was to stick to pure mathematics.

• • •

No one knew it at the time, but the butterfly effect would spawn a new branch of mathematics called chaos theory, with applications in many fields beyond meteorology. Indeed, chaos theory would be one of the most important scientific revolutions of the twentieth century. And Margaret, in her first job as a programmer, armed with her sharp pencil and Scotch tape, had been there at its start.

THE BUTTERFLY EFFECT

The idea of the butterfly effect is that a butterfly flapping its wings sets off tiny eddies in the atmosphere. These trigger an ever-growing cascade of events that theoretically can grow into a dramatic change in the weather, even a tornado. On the other hand, they could just as easily *prevent* a tornado. You can't predict.

And that's what Lorenz's rounding discrepancy had shown him when he was running Margaret's program. An insignificant change in the initial conditions leads to a completely different result. And since it's impossible to keep track of *all* the

A monarch butterfly takes off . . .

Weeks later, given countless other disruptions in the atmosphere, a tornado forms.

initial conditions—to account for every flap of a butterfly's wings or other atmospheric disturbance—it's impossible to have a truly long-range weather forecast beyond a week or two, no matter how good the starting data.

Even so, one to two weeks is far better than the two to four days attainable with the old style of forecasting, which relied on historical records and a weather forecaster's knack for "reading" the atmosphere.

The butterfly effect applies in many different fields, and it has even caught on in popular culture. Stories about time travel are especially attracted to the concept, since a person going back in time to experience a historic event inevitably disturbs things in minor ways that snowball out of control and transform world history—at least in the stories. Many philosophers believe this problem makes time travel out of the question. It is impossible to go back into the past without changing it, and the past by definition doesn't change.

This is just the kind of topic that Margaret and her father loved discussing.

Margaret and a colleague at the XD-1
control console on April 19, 1962.

CHAPTER 11

TWO NEW COMPUTERS

MARGARET'S NEXT JOB WAS A GIGANTIC UPGRADE from the LGP-30, which was one of the smallest computers of its day. She landed a spot as a programmer on the prototype of the 250-ton AN/FSQ-7, the largest computer ever built, called the Q7 for short. The initial version of this behemoth was designated the XD-1, and it was Margaret's machine—or rather the one she shared with a large team of other programmers. The XD-1 occupied one-half acre of office space and performed a blistering seventy-five thousand instructions per second, while consuming up to three million watts of electricity—enough to power thousands of homes.

The Q7's mission was air defense, a crucial national need after World War II, which had spawned nuclear weapons and jet aircraft to deliver them. Mounting a sneak attack, Soviet bombers could hypothetically fly over the North Pole and obliterate American cities and military bases with nuclear bombs before U.S. defenders had a chance to respond. Early warning was therefore crucial, and the U.S. Air Force created a system called SAGE, the Semi-Automatic Ground Environment. "Semi-automatic" meant that humans and machines worked together. The activities of thousands of military command and control personnel would be augmented for the first time by computers, which would collect radar data at lightning speed and guide antiaircraft defenses. It was a daunting task, requiring a network of giant radar dishes along with data processing machines of unprecedented size and power. Data processing was the Q7's job, and twenty-four command centers around the country would each be equipped with this colossus. The XD-1 that Margaret was hired to help program was supposed to prove that SAGE would work, as it ultimately did.

A Soviet bomber during the Cold War.

● ● ●

Like the Whirlwind computer on which it was based, the Q7 was a product of MIT engineering. This was true not only of the gargantuan machine itself but also of its intricate software, which was the responsibility of MIT's Lincoln Laboratory, located in the Boston suburbs. In early 1961, the lab's contractors began running ads looking for experienced programmers. These notices appeared in the job listings for men and declared "Salaries Open!" to entice applicants, since experienced programmers were rare.

At the time, a salary increase was just what Margaret needed. Jim was still in school, having switched from a PhD program in chemistry to Harvard Law School, which was more appealing to his commitment to improve society. Their daughter, Lauren, was a little over a year old and being looked after during the day by a babysitter. Meanwhile, Margaret's position with Professor Lorenz earned her only a student's wages. She loved working for the selfless and distinguished meteorologist, who was as much a hero to her as Florence Long, but she had to put her family's needs first. Reluctantly but with the thrill of embarking on a new adventure, she seized the chance to get a professional's salary on a challenging, high-priority national defense project.

When she called the recruiting firm, a shocked man told her that no woman had ever applied for a software-writing position. "I've never interviewed a girl before" is how he put it. Still, he agreed to talk to her, but he didn't want to interview her in the hotel room that his office had booked for screening applicants—all men, of course. That would look improper. So he arranged to meet her in the hotel bar. On arriving, Margaret found that the lounge had a ring-shaped counter with a bartender standing in the middle. Tables were arrayed around the bar on what was an actual working merry-go-round, rotating once every hour. It was an unusual place for a job interview, but Margaret was hired.

Merry-Go-Round Bar in Boston.

• • •

So many programmers were needed for the Q7 that Lincoln Lab sent each group of new employees to an out-of-town training program lasting six weeks, where they learned the computer's special language. Since Margaret didn't want to leave Lauren for so long, she convinced her boss to let her stay at the lab and teach herself. She assured him that she would do at least as well as the top student in the program.

The XD-1 control station shown on page 82, but three years earlier, on April 10, 1959. Everything visible is just a small part of the mammoth XD-1.

So she set to work learning the code, and when her group returned she was true to her word, proving her expertise and also solving a very special problem.

Before Margaret arrived, a tricky programmer named Ernie had worked on SAGE and then moved to another project, leaving behind pages of handwritten code that no one could understand. The lab even hired people to make sense of it, but no one could. So they asked Margaret. She read over Ernie's enigmatic code and said to herself, "I think I know what this does." She punched her translation of the program into a stack of cards and fed the cards into the reader on the XD-1. Then she waited . . .

"It's running! It's running!" she exclaimed as the printer typed furiously, producing text in Latin and Greek together with calculations for calibrating radars. The Latin and Greek were Ernie's little joke to throw off his colleagues. Staff came running over to see what was happening and learned that Margaret had cracked Ernie's riddle. In ancient legend, Arthur showed he was the true king of Britain by pulling the sword Excalibur from a chunk of rock. Margaret had done something similar with Ernie's baffling scribbles, proving she had mastered the Q7's difficult language.

Margaret's boss's boss was so impressed that he decided he wanted her to write code for *him*. Embarrassed, Margaret told her supervisors not to fight over her; she would write code for both. She eventually added a third client, doing programming for a group of radio astronomers at a nearby air force research lab. She was a very busy coder.

. . .

The sword-in-the-stone problem and other whimsical tests were part of the sometimes playful, always competitive, almost exclusively male spirit that was taking over computing. The machines were so much fun, even when programmers were working on sobering problems like thwarting nuclear attack, that a new culture was emerging that treated the computer as an endlessly entertaining toy. The age of creative computer tinkerers, or hackers, had arrived.

Margaret worked on the SAGE project for two years. Then she moved back to a programming job at the MIT meteorology department so she could be closer to her family in Cambridge. Returning to the problem of understanding the weather, she mastered a new computer called the PDP-1, which was the size of three refrigerators and even faster than the Q7. She shared the PDP-1 with users in other departments, including a group of MIT undergraduates—all male—who rarely went to class and programmed the machine to play games, produce eerie music, generate psychedelic art, and break into the global telephone system so that they could make free phone calls anywhere in the world.

Margaret hardly noticed these smart, if lawless, idlers until one day her code ran into a problem. It was considered immature to blame the computer in such situations, since the fault was almost always with the programmer. But Margaret knew her code was error free. So she approached the computer's supervisor. "I think something is wrong with the PDP-1," she said.

"It's your software," he replied curtly.

"No, it's the computer."

Indeed, the night before the hackers had surreptitiously rewired a couple of circuits in the PDP-1 in pursuit of one of their mischievous projects, confident that they could cover their tracks.

But Margaret had found them out. She was as much of a hacker as they were.

The MIT Instrumentation Laboratory, birthplace of the Apollo Guidance Computer and its software.

PART 2

COUNTDOWN

ENGINEERS

INSTRUMENTATION LABORATORY

The Laboratory, with a record of distinguished achievement in the field of guidance and control, has overall design responsibility for the complete guidance-navigation system for the Apollo project of manned flight to the moon. A number of openings exist with Apollo and other vital programs of the Laboratory for degree technical personnel with proven records of accomplishment. The Laboratory, adjacent to the main complex of MIT, offers an excellent environment for the individual interested in research. Compensation and benefits are attractive and competitive.

Apollo Field Assignments at Houston, Cape Kennedy, Los Angeles; Bethpage, L.I.

- TEST DIRECTORS to provide liaison and coordination with other contractors and technical direction of system and sub-system test activities. Minimum requirement of BS degree and 4 years experience.
- OPTICAL ENGINEER to assist in solving technical problems arising out of the installation and operation problems arising out of the installation and operation BS and 4 years experience.
- INERTIAL ENGINEERS to assist in solving technical problems arising out of the installation and operation of the inertial sub-system. Minimum requirement of BS and 4 years experience.
- COMPUTER ENGINEERS to assist in solving technical problems arising out of the installation and operation of the computer sub-system. Minimum requirement of BS and 4 years experience.

The following openings exist in Cambridge:

- DIGITAL SIMULATION ENGINEERS to participate in analysis and programming of digital simulation of Apollo guidance computer and spacecraft systems. Minimum requirement of BS degree and 2 years experience.
- COMPUTER PROGRAMMERS to assist in data processing, trajectory analysis, instrument data reduction and coding of flight programs. Minimum requirement of BS degree and 2 years experience.
- CIRCUIT DESIGNERS to design transistor circuits for inertial navigation system and develop electronic devices utilizing semi-conductors. Minimum requirement of BS degree and 4 years experience.
- ANALYSTS to perform analysis of flight control systems for large space boosters and re-entry vehicles. Minimum requirement of MS degree and 4 years experience.
- CHEMICAL ENGINEER to carry out materials research and chemical analyses necessary for design of advanced navigation instruments. Minimum requirement of MS degree and formal training in the areas of fluid mechanics and polymeric materials.
- CHEMIST to assist inertial instrumentation design group on polymer fluids, epoxy potting compounds, lubrication and material technology problems. Minimum requirement of BS degree and 1 year experience
- RELIABILITY ANALYST to handle apportionment, prediction and assessment based on legitimate statistical and mathematical approaches. Minimum requirement of BS degree and 2 years experience.

Address resume to PROFESSIONAL PLACEMENT

INSTRUMENTATION LABORATORY
MASSACHUSETTS INSTITUTE OF TECHNOLOGY
68 ALBANY STREET, BLDG. 10G, CAMBRIDGE 39, MASS.
Graduate courses may be taken while earning full pay
An equal opportunity employer

MASSACHUSETTS INSTITUTE OF TECHNOLOGY

The arrow points to the ad that led Margaret to her role in sending humans to the Moon.

CHAPTER 12
THE AD

IN THE FALL OF 1964, BOSTON NEWSPAPERS WERE full of news about the U.S. presidential election, China's first nuclear test, and the sudden change of leadership in the Soviet Union. There were also seasonal ads for Halloween costumes, winter clothing, and holiday gifts, plus job listings.

In those days, jobs were classified as either "male" or "female," even though the recently passed Civil Rights Act of 1964 outlawed discrimination in employment based on sex—also race, color, religion, and national origin. The new law didn't take full effect until the following year, and most newspapers stuck to sex classifications for the time being.

On three different days in October and November, a large ad appeared in the *Boston Globe* under the heading "Instrumentation Laboratory." Sharing the page were postings for welders, mechanics, night watchmen, and other occupations—all listed in the male section. The Instrumentation Lab was a renowned research center at MIT, and the ad boldly announced that the center had "overall design responsibility for the complete guidance-navigation system for the Apollo project of manned flight to the moon." It went on to describe several openings in technical fields, including computer programming.

Jim noticed the ad and showed it to Margaret. She was finally gearing up to go to graduate school in mathematics, but the announcement offered a once-in-a-lifetime opportunity. She immediately applied. "I thought that was very exciting—to work on a project to go to the moon," she said later. It was almost like science fiction. As usual, the fact that the ad seemed to be looking for men didn't deter her.

● ● ●

At the Instrumentation Lab (known as the IL), she had two interviews for two different positions. Both IL men saw that she was exceptionally well-qualified in computer programming. After covering this aspect of her career, they each asked about an item on her résumé that caught their attention. "Tell me about this job at the Arcadian Copper Mine," they queried her independently. So Margaret enthusiastically described her teenage career as Arvo's right-hand woman. They were genuinely impressed by her rapid rise from a junior tour guide to a business-savvy entrepreneur and manager. Technical people are notoriously solitary, and perhaps the two realized that this woman could do more than the computer coding described in the ad. With luck, she could be a leader. They both wanted her.

In fact, they fought over her—just as her bosses at Lincoln Lab had. She was given the choice of either writing software for a large computer at the IL, which would stay firmly earthbound but be instrumental to the project, much like the computers she had coded for Lorenz and on the SAGE project. Or she could join the team that was creating instructions for the miniature computer designed to travel to the Moon with the astronauts, assisting in writing what was called the onboard flight software. Unlike Lorenz's desk-sized LGP-30, this computer would be fully portable—about the size of a suitcase. At the time, this was considered unbelievably, perhaps impossibly, small. Working on such a marvel sounded so exciting and difficult that Margaret couldn't help being tempted. However, she didn't want to hurt anyone's feelings, so she told her interviewers that *they* should decide. Whether by coin toss or some other method, Margaret got the assignment she wanted: She would help code the Apollo Guidance Computer—the AGC—the revolutionary machine that would conduct astronauts to the Moon and back.

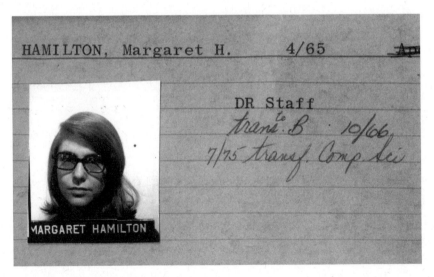

Margaret's employee card at the IL.

In 1964, the AGC hardware—the actual computer—was far along in development. But the onboard flight software was just taking shape. Margaret would be one of the first to wrestle with this daunting problem.

Margaret's work on SAGE had immersed her in the military standoff between the United States and the Soviet Union. Now she was about to get involved in a more peaceful aspect of the Cold War: the space race.

Ever since Sputnik was launched when she was a senior at Earlham, the Soviets and Americans had been exploring space with enthusiasm—both because it was an interesting thing to do and because it impressed the rest of the world. To the Soviets, dazzling other nations was a way to spread the communist ideology. If their socialist system could break the bonds of Earth and venture out into the cosmos, who knew what it could do for other countries? By contrast, U.S. officials saw space achievements as proof of the advantages of democracy and a free market. As Professor Trueblood at Earlham put it: "We accept the challenge to show which system is best ... We have reason to believe that a society which permits freedom of thought is, in the long run, more productive." And not just in science and technology, the professor asserted, but also in art, general culture, and "the well-being of the total population."

On May 25, 1961, these considerations led President John F. Kennedy to announce the goal of landing a man on the Moon by the end of the decade. The Soviets had already been first to launch a satellite in 1957, the first to hit the Moon with an automatic probe in 1959, and the first to launch a human into orbit around the Earth in April 1961. Kennedy's advisers told him that the Soviets would continue to be first in space for the foreseeable future, thanks to their head start in heavy-lift rockets. However, if he picked a goal that was far ahead of existing technology, something that was almost unbelievably difficult, then the United States stood a good chance of coming in first.

So Kennedy decided to go to the Moon. And Margaret—along with four hundred thousand other people who would eventually work on the Apollo program—was part of the team.

The rocket that gave the Soviet Union its head start in space. Versions of this vehicle launched the first satellite, the first probe to hit the Moon, the first human to orbit the Earth, and many other space missions.

The Pleiades, a prominent star cluster traditionally used by sailors for navigation.

CHAPTER 13

THE AGC

IN HIS SPEECH ANNOUNCING THE APOLLO PRO-
gram, Kennedy stressed that no space project would be so difficult to
accomplish. His listeners were surely picturing giant rockets, mammoth launch facilities, spidery landing craft, and other futuristic
components that had yet to be built.

Very few were thinking about an equally vital element: the guidance and control system that would tell the astronauts where they
were in their long journey, where they wanted to be, and how to get
there.

The guidance and control system was so crucial that it was given
top priority. And James E. Webb, the head of the National Aeronautics and Space Administration, knew exactly who he wanted to
build it: Charles Stark "Doc" Draper of MIT's Instrumentation Laboratory. Doc and his engineers had designed remarkable guidance
systems for the army, navy, and air force, and Webb immediately
lined them up to do the same for Apollo.

• • •

After getting the contract, IL engineers spent the next few months defining exactly what was needed to perform their part of the mission. First, the Apollo spacecraft had to have an inertial measurement unit (IMU) to keep track of the vehicle's position. "Inertial" refers to the tendency of a moving object to keep going in its current state: to stay spinning if it's spinning, or traveling in a straight line if that's what it's doing. You can think of an object in an inertial state as "minding its own business," primed to detect any deviation from that state. In the case of the IMU, the moving, inertial object was a spinning disk, called a gyroscope, mounted so that its supporting frame could rotate in any direction. Amazingly, this simple device can detect if a vehicle is pushed up or down, turned right or left, or rotated sideways. It does this because any force acting on the spinning disk creates a corresponding force on the frame. And that force can be measured.

In addition to several gyroscopes, the IMU had accelerometers. These use an inertial sensor to measure changes in velocity—whether the unit is speeding up or slowing down. Together, the gyroscopes and accelerometers act like eyes and ears (ears in the sense of the inner ear, which the body uses for balance), telling the spacecraft where it is in space and how it is oriented.

Because tiny inaccuracies in the IMU eventually grow into major errors, the vehicle's coordinates (the numbers indicating its location in space) must be updated periodically. For this, the IL team designed a sextant and scanning telescope that astronauts could use to observe selected stars and determine the ship's exact position, just like sailors at sea. These coordinates would then be entered into the IMU to keep the spacecraft's position data accurate.

• • •

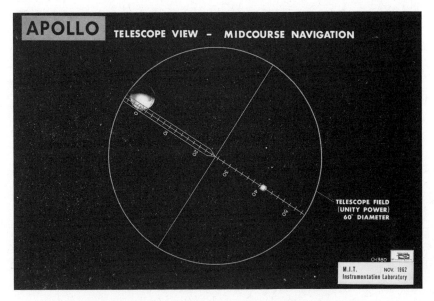

The view through Apollo's sextant allowed an astronaut to measure the angle between two celestial objects: here, the limb of the Earth and a bright star. The AGC used this number and other data to determine the spacecraft's exact position.

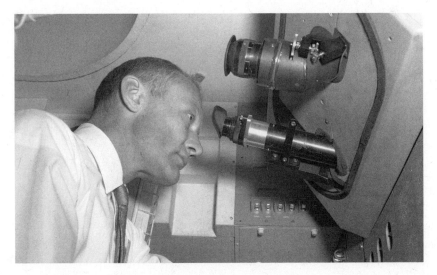

Astronaut Buzz Aldrin at the eyepieces of the IL's space sextant.

So far, so good. However, the task of navigating through space, calculating and timing rocket firings, and keeping track of the spacecraft's many subsystems (electrical power, oxygen, and communications, among others) was so complicated that the three astronauts aboard an Apollo mission couldn't possibly manage it by themselves. For this, they needed an onboard computer, the Apollo Guidance Computer, or AGC. The trouble was, no computer so small, so versatile, and so efficient had ever been built. The problem was one of the most difficult of the entire Apollo program, and it was up to the IL to solve it.

As Doc Draper and his engineers got started on this electronic wonder in 1961, they didn't realize that an even bigger problem loomed. Writing the programs for the AGC would be far more complicated than anyone ever imagined. Three years later, in 1964, that realization led to the ad that Margaret saw in the *Boston Globe*. And *that* led her to the most challenging and rewarding assignment of her life.

DOC GETS THE JOB

Aboard Air Force One, Jim Webb (left) and Doc Draper (center) confer with President Lyndon B. Johnson.

During World War II, Doc Draper's lab at MIT produced gyroscopic aiming devices for antiaircraft guns under contract to a company managed by a go-getting lawyer named Jim Webb. Webb was so dazzled by Doc's work that twenty years later when Webb was head of NASA, he went to Doc to sound him out about the guidance system for Apollo. According to Doc, the conversation went like this:

Webb, *getting down to business*: Doc, you know we have to build a spacecraft to go to the Moon?

Doc: Yes.

Webb: I think that the guidance system is one of our hardest problems. Do you think that you could help us with that?

Doc, *confidently*: Yes, of course.

Webb: Well, when would the system be ready?

Doc, *bragging*: It would be ready when you need it.

Webb: And how will I know if it will work?

Doc, *dead serious*: I'll volunteer to go along and fly it for you to the Moon!

Doc got the job. He also applied to join the astronaut corps. He was not joking about operating his own equipment wherever it happened to be. But at age sixty, he was deemed too old, among other disqualifications, which included his lack of test pilot experience.

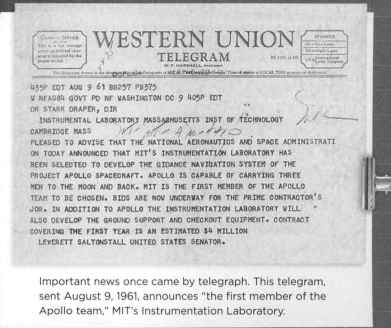

Important news once came by telegraph. This telegram, sent August 9, 1961, announces "the first member of the Apollo team," MIT's Instrumentation Laboratory.

Too old to be an astronaut himself, Doc courted thrills behind the wheel of his British sports car.

An astronaut operates the display and keyboard (DSKY) on the command module's control panel, communicating directly with the Apollo Guidance Computer.

CHAPTER 14

THE PROGRAM

A SOFTWARE PROGRAM IS A LIST OF INSTRUC-
tions to accomplish a task. Let's say the task is making chocolate chip
cookies. First you need a shopping list. You look up a recipe and write
down:

> flour
>
> brown sugar
>
> white sugar
>
> chocolate chips
>
> walnuts
>
> butter
>
> eggs
>
> vanilla
>
> salt
>
> baking soda

But instead of heading to the store yourself, you want a robot to do
the shopping. This robot has none of the background knowledge that
humans have, so you have to give it more information, such as:

1. Directions to the store
2. How to enter the store
3. The aisle and shelf where each item is located
4. The order to follow in getting the items
5. Substitutions (for example, pecans if walnuts aren't available)
6. How to pay for the items
7. How to exit the store
8. Directions home

The robot also needs other guidance. What if the payment card isn't accepted? What if the store is closed? What if there's an emergency (say, the store loses power)? Each of these and many other contingencies must be programmed in advance. And that's just for the shopping. Assembling the ingredients and baking the cookies require a different program with even more instructions.

Furthermore, these commands are in English—a language that it took most of us our formative years to learn. How do you convey these concepts to a collection of electronic circuits? And if making chocolate chip cookies is so complicated, what about guiding and controlling a mission to the Moon?

● ● ●

One reason it took the Instrumentation Lab three years to get around to hiring Margaret and a host of other programmers was that the role of the AGC was simple to begin with but kept expanding—like a shopping list that grows as the scope of a meal becomes clear. What was originally supposed to be a single computer navigating a single spacecraft to the Moon and back became *two* computers with a much more complicated mission.

The original Apollo plan was for a gigantic rocket to take off from Earth and propel a human-carrying spacecraft directly to a landing on the Moon. After the astronauts explored the surface, the vehicle would return straight to Earth. There were several problems with this approach. First, the rocket would have to be far larger than anything considered practical at the time. Second, the spacecraft itself would need to be so big that it would be difficult to maneuver to a landing on the Moon. And third, hitting a specific spot on the Moon would require flawless guidance from Earth—like sinking a basketball through a moving hoop at a distance of seven miles.

All of these problems could be solved by breaking the spacecraft into two parts: a mother ship (called the command module, or CM) and a small lander (called the lunar module, or LM, usually pronounced "lem"). Instead of a direct flight, the combined spacecraft would proceed by stages:

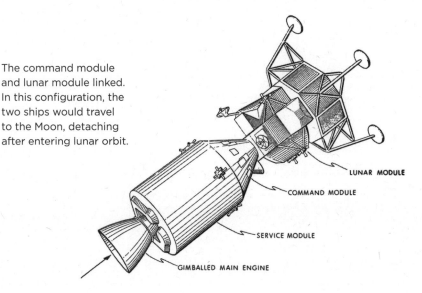

The command module and lunar module linked. In this configuration, the two ships would travel to the Moon, detaching after entering lunar orbit.

LUNAR MODULE

COMMAND MODULE

SERVICE MODULE

GIMBALLED MAIN ENGINE

1. The attached CM and LM are launched into Earth orbit by a single rocket.
2. After all systems are checked, the CM and LM then proceed to the Moon.
3. The CM and LM (still attached) go into orbit around the Moon.
4. Two astronauts climb aboard the LM; it detaches from the CM (where the third astronaut stays behind), and the LM descends to the Moon.
5. The two astronauts explore the Moon.
6. The LM rockets back into lunar orbit to rejoin the CM.
7. The LM is discarded, and the CM with all three astronauts heads back to Earth.

By breaking up the journey this way, a less gargantuan rocket would suffice for launch. Also, the new plan allowed a much smaller lander that could be easily maneuvered, avoiding the difficulty of backing a large ship onto the Moon. Finally, guidance would be much more flexible, since the trajectory could be adjusted in Earth orbit, on the way to the Moon, and further fine-tuned in lunar orbit. The original plan, called direct ascent, could be compared to a cross-country trip in a full-sized passenger bus. By contrast, the new plan, called lunar-orbit rendezvous, was like making the same trip in a small camper van, taking along a motor scooter for side excursions. Lunar-orbit rendezvous had the advantages of being more efficient, adaptable, and less costly.

• • •

On the other hand, these advantages came at the expense of much greater software complexity. The CM and LM each required their

Guided by its own onboard computer, the lunar module would descend to the Moon. Only the top section, above the landing legs, would later ascend to rejoin the orbiting command module.

own computer with software tailored to the needs of that particular spacecraft—not just for navigation but also for running flight instruments, autopilots, thrusters, and rocket engines. Never before had a computer been in charge of such vital functions on a flying machine, let alone *two* flying machines operating in tandem.

Another Apollo innovation was called "fly-by-wire." Usually, cables, gears, hydraulics, and other mechanical parts responded to the pilot's control input in a flying machine. But on Apollo the astronauts' commands would travel entirely by wire, via electronic signals sent by the computer. This was done to save weight. However, it made the astronauts very nervous. They had never trusted their lives to a computer before.

Yet another requirement was that the astronauts had to be able to operate the computer with near-instantaneous results, which was not how most computers at the time worked. The usual lengthy process of writing out instructions by hand, converting them into punch cards, delivering the cards to a computer technician, and then often waiting overnight for the results—as Margaret had done with the XD-1—would never do for a mission to the Moon. Instead, IL engineers designed a simple display and keyboard that the crew could use

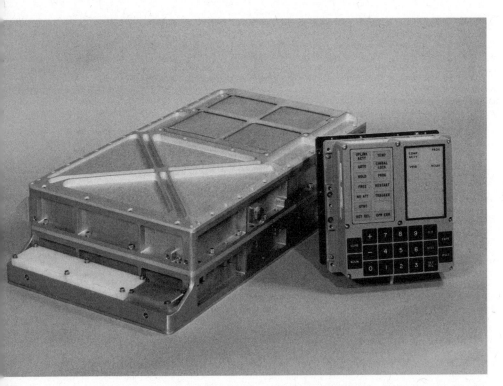

AGC and DSKY. The AGC is two feet long.

to give commands directly to the computer. Looking like an over-size electronic calculator, the display and keyboard were abbreviated DSKY, pronounced "diskey." Rather than punching holes in cards, the astronauts would type a few numbers into the DSKY, hit some operations keys, and the spacecraft would respond promptly by firing a rocket, maneuvering to a new position, or performing some other assignment. If this type of input device sounds familiar, it is only because the AGC and its DSKY paved the way for easy communication between a human and a computer.

An especially nerve-racking aspect of the AGC was that the hardware, software, and DSKY had to work perfectly. There would be no time to fix a malfunction in space. Computer error was not an option.

• • •

The IL's head of Apollo Mission Development, Richard Battin, was getting indigestion thinking about all these requirements. In the beginning, he had no more than five programmers to write code for the AGC. Programming was an art, and he felt that more people would get in one another's way. To make his point, he liked to tell an apocryphal story about Michelangelo's frescoes for the Sistine Chapel ceiling in Rome. The work was going so slowly that Michel-angelo's client, the pope, suggested hiring a team of housepainters to speed up the work. Naturally, the great artist thought this was a terrible idea.

Battin felt the same way about computer code. It was an art that could not be rushed. Even so, he had to do something. One day he confided to a colleague that he was thinking of asking for more help.

"Well, how many people do you think you need?" the colleague asked.

"I might need twenty or thirty," said Battin.

The man was shocked. "Twenty or thirty people? What would you do with them?!"

In the end, Battin had to hire more than four hundred.

ADA, COUNTESS OF LOVELACE

Is thy face like thy mother's, my fair child!
Ada! sole daughter of my house and of my heart?
When last I saw thy young blue eyes they smiled,
And then we parted.

So wrote England's most notorious Romantic poet, Lord Byron, in 1816 after his wife left him, taking their infant daughter, Ada. He never saw Ada again. As Ada grew up, her mother insisted that she study mathematics in hopes it would steer her away from her father's wild, undisciplined ways. The strategy worked, giving the world its first computer programmer.

As a young woman, the logic-loving Ada mingled with innovative thinkers in Britain who were transforming science and technology. One in particular, Charles Babbage, planned to build what he called an Analytical Engine, capable of performing any calculation that could be programmed on a set of punch cards, which had been invented to automate looms for weaving complex patterns in cloth. In short, the Analytical Engine was to be a general-purpose computer,

Ada, about age twenty-five.

a century before its time. Ada fell in love with the idea and convinced Babbage to let her collaborate on the project.

Her key contribution was to figure out how programs should work and to write one with all the features of a modern computer program, such as recursive loops, subroutines, conditional branching, and commentary. Even though Babbage never built his Analytical Engine, Ada's complete documentation of a sample set of instructions makes her the forerunner of today's software engineers.

Now recognized as a trailblazer, Ada is honored with the Ada Lovelace Award, given by the Association of Women in Computing for outstanding achievement in technical work and for extraordinary service on behalf of women in computing. The award went to Margaret Hamilton in 1986 for her contributions to the Apollo program.

Modern reconstruction of a calculating unit for one of Babbage's computers.

Astronaut Alan Shepard signs in at the IL's security desk, 1962.

CHAPTER 15
THE IL

MARGARET FELT RIGHT AT HOME AS SOON AS SHE walked in the door at 75 Cambridge Parkway, the building where work on the AGC was underway. The three floors of busy engineers radiated the thrill she had known at Lorenz's lab and on the SAGE project, but to a heightened degree. After all, the Instrumentation Laboratory was creating a device that would guide humans to the Moon. It was a top-priority national effort in which all that mattered was solving problems and solving them quickly, regardless of one's title, credentials, or sex. It was the perfect environment for a woman brought up to be curious, diligent, fearless, and a bit of a rebel.

A guard at the entrance checked her newly issued security badge. She had also had a security clearance on SAGE. There, it was obvious you weren't supposed to talk about your classified defense work. But here it was different. Unlike the supersecret Soviet space program, Apollo was being conducted in the open. On the other hand, since certain aspects of its technology had military applications, a degree of secrecy prevailed. As she walked down the hall, signs warned, "Don't Chatter Classified Matter." Other reminders were red padlocked trash cans labeled "Classified Waste Only."

On balance, the atmosphere at the IL was informal and collegial. Margaret shared her first office with a group of engineers who kept a pet iguana. The creature was a fascinating diversion for Lauren whenever she came to visit. Only five years old when her mother started at the IL, Lauren had an imperfect understanding of what was going on. For example, she thought the managers at the IL never worked because they were always on the phone, something she associated with adults talking to their friends and relatives.

• • •

Number 75 Cambridge Parkway had once been the headquarters for a popular brand of underwear and hosiery. Such industries had mostly left that part of Cambridge, where the sewing machine, telephone, radar, frozen orange juice, and automated candy production had all been perfected. An aroma of peppermint and chocolate still filled the

75 Cambridge Parkway during its heyday in hosiery.

The MIT campus from the Boston side of the
Charles River. The IL building is at the far right.

air near the New England Confectionery Company (Necco), makers of Necco Wafers, but other factory buildings surrounding the MIT campus were vacant. This made it easy to find parking spaces close to the IL. On the other hand, the neighborhood was spooky late at night when many of the staff were just finishing their day's work.

The old underwear warehouse looked out on the Charles River. Upstream was MIT's main campus, and around the bend was Harvard University. Directly across the water was the city of Boston with its gold-domed State House and a single skyscraper, the Prudential Tower, which proud citizens bragged was the tallest building on the continent of North America—if New York City's Manhattan Island was not counted as part of the continent.

Beyond Boston, just three miles from the IL, was Logan International Airport, where passenger planes could be seen gently ascending and descending over the skyline. IL staff were often aboard those planes, leaving and returning from trips to NASA centers and contractors all around the country.

• • •

One of Margaret's first assignments was mastering the inertial measurement unit and the coordinate system used to guide Apollo to the Moon. Coordinates specify a point in space, such as latitude and longitude on a two-dimensional map. For the three dimensions of a lunar trip, an additional number is needed, such as altitude. The IMU would keep track of these changing coordinates through every phase of the mission.

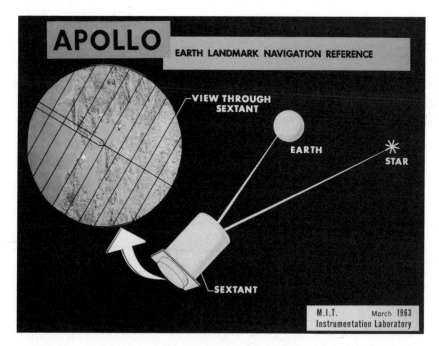

Landmark tracking was one way to determine the position of the spacecraft. Here, the landmark is San Francisco Bay. Lunar landmarks were also used.

To give her practice with actual code, Margaret was asked to write software that would let astronauts orbiting the Moon determine their position by sighting on prominent craters below. When a mission with this software eventually flew, some engineers were in a panic, convinced that Margaret had entered the data "upside down and backwards."

"I almost had a heart attack," Margaret recalled. "But I was right. They were the ones who were upside down and backwards!" As her reputation spread, everyone at the IL learned to trust her completely.

Margaret concentrated on mastering the AGC's programming language. One assignment called for writing emergency instructions for the lunar module's descent engine in case it didn't produce enough thrust prior to a lunar landing. The LM's descent engine was designed to be simple and absolutely reliable, so failure was considered practically impossible. Margaret's code would almost surely never run during an actual mission, so her bosses thought it was a good training exercise for her.

Since code that performed a specific task was usually given a brief, descriptive name for identification, Margaret called her program FORGET IT. Its job was to pull the plug on the rocket engine, saying in essence, "Forget it!" There was a double meaning too, since everyone at the IL could "forget" this piece of code because it would never run.

Of course, when an actual mission flew several years later, it *did* run. And all hell broke loose.

The lunar module being prepared for its first unmanned test. The black nozzle of the descent propulsion system juts from the bottom of the spacecraft.

CHAPTER 16

FORGET IT

THE UNEXPECTED DEBUT OF "FORGET IT" OCCURRED during the first unmanned test of the lunar module and its specially programmed AGC.

On launch day, about twenty IL staff members, including Margaret, assembled in a third-floor room at the Instrumentation Lab. Called the SCAMA room (for switching, conference, and monitoring arrangement), the cluttered space was packed with tables, chairs, reference documents, chalkboards, and an intercom connected to NASA's Mission Control in Houston, where the flight was being managed.

The takeoff from Florida was flawless. Soon the lunar module was orbiting Earth, where it was to perform a series of rocket burns that simulated a lunar landing. With the software running the show, the AGC counted down to the moment of ignition for the descent propulsion system (called the DPS, pronounced "dips"). The DPS was the rocket that would power the astronauts' descent to the Moon. At zero, a voice from Houston relayed success over the intercom: "DPS on."

Everything was going like clockwork.

The SCAMA room during an Apollo mission. Margaret is partially visible at the extreme right, wearing a headset.

Suddenly, the voice said, "Program caution!" Then, "DPS off!" The engine had unexpectedly quit.

At Mission Control, someone else announced two computer alarms, including FORGET IT.

"What's FORGET IT?" thought practically everyone.

Except Margaret. She was thinking: "I hope this is not a mistake!"

• • •

Doc Draper was following the flight from the launch center in Florida. He was just as confused by the engine failure as anyone. Strictly a hardware engineer, he looked uncomprehendingly at the FORGET IT code as an IL programmer explained that the LM contractor must have given MIT the wrong timing value. Meanwhile, a LM engineer was insisting that it was MIT's mistake.

Eventually, the cause was pinned down. Among the lander's

roughly one million parts were valves feeding propellants into the descent stage's combustion chamber. Prelaunch tests showed that some of these parts were prone to small leaks. The simplest fix was to delay opening the valves for 1.3 seconds after the "DPS on" command. This would prevent possible premature combustion, which might blow the engine apart. The change was made, but LM engineers neglected to tell the IL about it. Therefore when the mission flew and the DPS was switched on, the 1.3-second delay led the software to conclude that the engine had failed. And *that* triggered Margaret's FORGET IT program. The software behaved exactly as it should have, given the information available to the IL.

```
633436A YUL SYSTEM FOR AGC: REVISION 0 OF PROGRAM BURST123 BY NASA 2A21106-031        DEC 7, 1967  (MAIN)  PAGE 101

L       FRESH START AND RESTART                                          USER'S OWN PAGE NO.  14          53 E3

P2065   FAKESTRT IS ENTERED FROM GOPROG WHEN A RESTART OCCURS AND THE RESTARTABILITY FLAG IS OFF.

2075                              07,2000              BANK  7
2080    REF  3 LAST  94          07,2000  0 4755 1  FAKESTRT  TC   ALARM
2085                             07,2001  00316 0           OCT  0316       FAKESTRT ALARM

2090    REF  1                   07,2002  1 2014 1           TCF  FORGET2

R2095   FORGETIT IS ENTERED FROM:
R2100        1)  FAKESTRT (VIA FORGET2).
R2105        2)  VERB 74 UPLINK COMMAND.
R2110        3)  ILLEGAL MISSION PHASE COMES DUE IN MISSION SCHEDULING ROUTINE.
R2120        4)  ENGINE FAILURE, ETC.
R2125
2130                             07,2003  0 0004 0  DDV74   INHINT
2131    REF  4 LAST 100          07,2004  0 5270 1           TC   IBNKCALL
2132    REF  3 LAST 100          07,2005  02374 0           CADR  STARTSB2

2133    REF  2 LAST 101          07,2006  1 2014 1           TCF  FORGET2       BYPASS THE PROGRAM ALARM & 315 DISPLAY.

2135                             07,2007  0 0004 0  FORGETIT INHINT
2140    REF  5 LAST 101          07,2010  0 5270 1           TC   IBNKCALL
2145    REF  4 LAST 101          07,2011  02374 0           CADR  STARTSB2

2150    REF  4 LAST 101          07,2012  0 4755 1           TC   ALARM
2155                             07,2013  00315 0           OCT  315          UNIQUE ALARM FOR FORGETIT.

2160    REF  3 LAST 100          07,2014  0 6067 0  FORGET2  TC   FLAGDOWN     ENTRY FROM FAKESTRT.
2165                             07,2015  04000 0           OCT  0400N         KNOCK DOWN RESTART FLAG TO PERMIT POOH.

2170                             07,2016  0 0004 0           INHINT
2175                             07,2017  0 0006 1           EXTEND
2180    REF  1                   07,2020  3 2102 0           DCA  KILLPAD
2185    REF  1                   07,2021  53'075 0           DXCH DVMNEXIT

2190                             07,2022  0 0006 1           EXTEND
2195    REF  1                   07,2023  3 2100 1           DCA  CADAVER
2200    REF  4 LAST  67          07,2024  53'073 0           DXCH AVGEXIT

2205    REF  1                   07,2025  3 2076 1           CAF  PINGSMON
2207    REF  1                   07,2026  55'346 0           TS   OLDDVSEL
2210    REF  1                   07,2027  55'310 0           TS   DVSELECT

2215    REF  6 LAST 101          07,2030  0 5270 1           TC   IBNKCALL
2220    REF  1                   07,2031  40263 1           CADR ENGINOFF

2225    REF  7 LAST 101          07,2032  0 5270 1           TC   IBNKCALL
2230    REF  2 LAST 100          07,2033  40114 1           CADR STOPRATE
```

Margaret's FORGET IT program covers a few lines on page 101 of the lunar module's AGC code. The entire document is 1,285 pages long.

During the flight, Mission Control in Houston understood more or less what had happened—but not why. In scrambling to save the mission, they decided to switch off the AGC and run everything from the ground. This would not be practical during an actual manned lunar landing, but Flight Director Gene Kranz didn't want to jeopardize the mission's main goals, which were to test the LM's rocket engines and other mechanical components. The all-important tryout of the IL's software for the LM would have to wait.

Kranz had never heard of FORGET IT, and he was taken aback by its frivolous-sounding name, not to mention the mission-threatening

Flight Director Gene Kranz at Mission Control in Houston.

drama it unleashed. Afterward, he blamed the crisis on "an incorrect computer instruction." The chief engineer for the LM called it "a software error." A NASA documentary about the flight boasted, "The inability of an onboard computer to cope with a programming error was overcome by the infinitely more flexible mind of man."

In fact, the AGC was coping just fine. "Incorrect computer instruction," "inability to cope," "programming error"—these were the usual reactions to any problem involving computers. Movies like *Desk Set* spread this attitude among the general public. But people who should have known better were also influenced, including NASA controllers and even the astronaut corps.

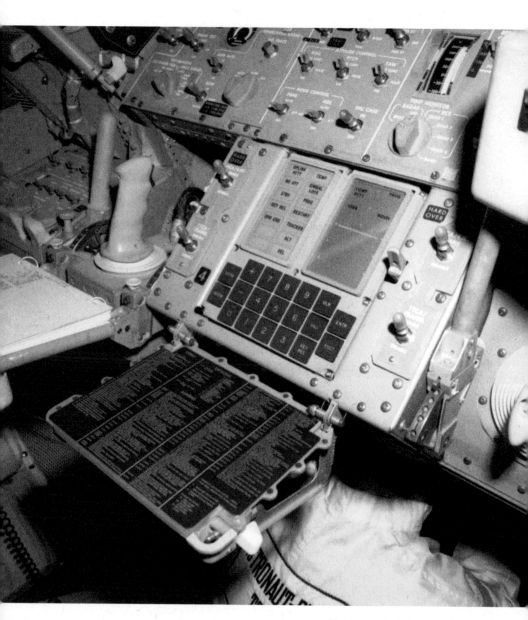

The DSKY installed in a lunar module. A directory of codes and commands is attached.

CHAPTER 17

THE ASTRONAUTS VERSUS THE AGC

AFTER MARGARET ARRIVED AT THE INSTRUMENTA-tion Lab, she rose rapidly through the organization, in part by identifying weak links in the software, such as interface errors. An interface error occurs when two or more parts don't interact correctly. A familiar example is ill-fitting shoes. The shoes are perfectly fine and so are your feet, but they don't work together as a unit. In the LM, a wrong timing value triggered the FORGET IT program. *That* was an interface error; the LM engine was working fine and so was the software, but they failed as a unit because of an incorrect piece of information.

The AGC and the Apollo spacecraft were rife with interfaces, and Margaret made it her mission to make these potential trouble spots work seamlessly, "like a finely tuned orchestra." In addition, she was soon responsible for hiring and training other programmers—much as she had done with the guides at Arvo's mine back in Michigan.

In due course, she was put in charge of more and more pieces of the software puzzle: first the system software that was common to both the command module and the lunar module; then that plus *all* the CM's specialized programs; then that plus *all* the LM's specialized programs—in other words, *all* onboard flight software, every line of code that was taking the astronauts to the Moon and back. That move up the management ladder would take Margaret a few years, but she was definitely on the road to leadership that her two interviewers had envisioned when she answered the *Boston Globe* ad.

Meanwhile, she was getting to know many of the future Moon voyagers as they came to the lab for meetings and training. One in particular caught the eye of her boss. "Who the hell was that guy up front?" he asked after a technical presentation. "Oh, that's Neil Armstrong," somebody said. Full of insightful questions and observations, Armstrong was obviously a talented engineer as well as one of the nation's top pilots. He would be a quick study on the AGC.

• • •

Most of the astronauts had engineering degrees, but that didn't guarantee enthusiasm about the AGC. After all, the computer was designed not just to guide the Apollo spacecraft but to *fly* it—a task the astronauts prided themselves on performing to perfection.

Ever since the invention of the airplane, engineers had been coming up with ways to automate flying. By the 1950s, when the Apollo astronauts were jet pilots in the military, their planes were typically equipped with autopilots that could maintain a specific course while also keeping the craft stable. But even with the autopilot engaged, the pilot always had manual control of the aircraft and plenty to do. Much of the pilot's training involved memorizing hundreds of dials and switches in the cockpit and knowing how to troubleshoot a bewildering number of

Astronauts Alan Shepard, Deke Slayton, John Glenn, and Scott Carpenter (left to right) outside the IL, 1962.

potential problems. There was a panel of warning lights to signal serious trouble, but the plane could not respond to a crisis on its own. That was the pilot's job, and dealing with large and small emergencies was a major part of what military flying was about.

For this reason, the astronauts were shocked to learn that Apollo would have a computer-controlled digital autopilot that would not just maintain the spacecraft's course and stability, much like a traditional mechanical autopilot, but would also do practically *all* the flying. This had never before been attempted in a piloted vehicle. Even astronaut David Scott, who had studied under IL engineers as a graduate student, had his doubts. He recounted that fellow astronauts delivered the following message to IL engineers: "You can't build a digital autopilot. Why don't you guys quit wasting time. Go back to MIT and think."

Part of Margaret's job was to help convince the astronauts that the IL knew what it was doing. Different phases of an Apollo mission were far too complex for full manual control of the vehicle, especially during a lunar landing. The computer *had* to be in charge. Eventually the astronauts realized that if any of them refused to fly with a digital autopilot, then a less picky astronaut would get the assignment. LM engineer Joseph Gavin had spent his career working with pilots and put it this way: "Inevitably, they will resist anything that's automatic. But you give them the first ten percent, and after it's been there a while you find that, by golly, they're using it. Then you give them another twenty percent. Pretty soon . . . they've built themselves a little stick with a rubber suction cup on the end so that they can put their seat back and work the dials on the autopilot with this little stick.

"You know, it's human nature," Gavin reflected. "They've been brought up to fly manually. If you gradually work in something that's automatic, they'll take it."

As astronauts slowly warmed to the idea of their multipurpose computer, they got involved in different aspects of it, taking particular interest in the DSKY—the display and keyboard. This device allowed them to communicate directly with the AGC and get almost instantaneous feedback. Using the DSKY was like giving orders in the military, a privilege familiar to all astronauts. The software might be doing the flying, but the astronauts would be issuing the commands, telling the computer to calculate and execute a precise rocket burn or perform some other task. Since they would be making thousands of DSKY keystrokes on a typical mission, they worked closely with Margaret and other programmers to figure out the most efficient procedures. Usually the astronauts wanted more performance from the AGC than its limited memory could provide, and these demands had to be negotiated in grueling daylong meetings at the IL, often followed by dinner at Doc Draper's favorite restaurant, Locke-Ober Café in Boston. Since Locke-Ober had a men-only policy, Margaret had to sneak into these after-hours gatherings.

Astronauts and engineers at an IL meeting in 1963. The arrow points at Neil Armstrong, sitting behind the astronaut with his chin on his hand.

• • •

While the astronauts might have grudgingly accepted the idea of the AGC, they were still on their guard. At one meeting before the customary Locke-Ober dinner, Margaret was running a mission simulation where she played the role of the pilot, operating the DSKY in a mock-up of the command module. At the perilous end of the flight, as the CM was reentering Earth's atmosphere, the system crashed and the screen suddenly went blank, as if the mission had ended in disaster. "I had forgotten to put in the correct data at the beginning of the run," Margaret later admitted. "The astronauts could not stop laughing. It was very bad timing."

Afterward at Locke-Ober, the future Moon voyagers wouldn't let Margaret forget that ominous blank screen.

Margaret monitors a practice lunar landing taking place in the adjoining lunar module simulator (see photo on page 138). Such simulations were vital for verifying software.

CHAPTER 18

"WHAT IF . . . ?"

MARGARET'S BIGGEST CONCERN WAS NOT KEEPING the astronauts happy but keeping them alive. There were many chances for error from the hardware, software, and the astronauts themselves. Mistakes that would be a nuisance in an earthbound computer could easily doom a crew in space, where something as common as a computer crash—where the AGC ceased to function—could literally crash the ship. "I used to stay awake at night worrying about this," Margaret remembered. As a mathematician, she approached the issue as rationally as she could, asking herself "What if . . . ?" for an almost endless list of emergencies.

It was while pondering these perils that she decided the software should be able to interrupt an astronaut in the middle of doing something on the DSKY and announce a pressing matter that needed immediate attention. She called the interruption a priority display since the top priority was now responding to the crisis. It would be like a waiter telling a diner in the middle of a meal that a fire had broken out in the kitchen, requiring prompt evacuation. "I wanted to have the software talk to the astronaut, which was a crazy idea at the time," she said.

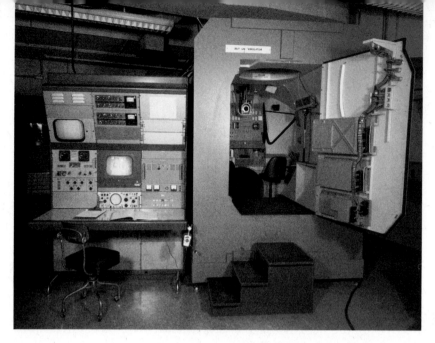

Up the steps and through the door is the IL's duplicate of the lunar module cockpit, used for training astronauts and testing new code and procedures.

She figured out how the software could do this and called a meeting of hardware and mission experts.

"It's impossible to do what you're trying to do," they told her.

"Why?" she asked.

"Because the DSKY is off more than it's on during a mission."

"Why can't it be left on all the time?" she countered.

"Because the hardware might wear out."

That sounded unlikely for the relatively short duration of an Apollo flight. Indeed, the engineers thought about it for a few days and then decided that Margaret was right.

"I will never forget," she later said, "how much it meant to me for them not only to give it serious consideration, but to decide in favor of changing the hardware design ... especially since it would have a direct impact on everyone including the astronauts."

These men who seemed so much older than she was—by three or four years at least—were taking her seriously.

. . .

But that was not her only hurdle.

"It will never work," another panel of experts told her about her idea.

"Why not?" she asked.

"Because the software won't know which display the astronaut is responding to, the original display or the new display." Their worry was that the switchover to the emergency program would lag the priority display by a second or two, so that an astronaut who reacted too quickly might get a "normal" response instead of the emergency alternative.

Margaret mulled this over for a day or two and came up with a simple answer. After getting the priority display, the astronaut would count to five before taking any action. Then he would know that the software was running the emergency routine.

The more that experts thought about priority display, the more sense it made. After Mission Control managers and the astronauts looked it over, they adopted Margaret's plan enthusiastically.

. . .

Priority display was just one step in a process that Margaret called error detection and recovery in real time—that is, as the mission is happening. She wanted the software to be able to detect a mission-critical error, alert the crew by interrupting them with a priority display telling them what was wrong, and then recover as many of the normal functions as possible. Whether or not all normal functions returned would depend on the seriousness of the problem and the actions taken by the astronauts in response to the emergency. The important thing was that the software would recover its most crucial functions on its own and not crash. The system was a lot like a circuit breaker in a house. When a wire short-circuits, the breaker instantly closes, shutting off electrical current and preventing an overheated wire and a possible fire. The breaker is called a "fail-safe" mechanism because it responds to a failure by automatically triggering a safe condition. Margaret's system was more flexible than this, as if a breaker could go halfway, reverting to a safe state while allowing some current to still flow.

Part of what she and her team did to accomplish this was to rank every function in the software according to its importance relative to all the other functions. In a process called priority scheduling, the software engineers manually assigned a priority number to each section of code, from the most critical to the least. Think about the shopping list for chocolate chip cookies from chapter 14. If you went to the store and discovered you didn't have enough money for all the ingredients, you could prioritize the list and only purchase those items that were absolutely necessary—say, flour, white sugar, chocolate chips, butter, and eggs. Although the final product might not be as tasty, you could leave out the brown sugar, walnuts, vanilla, salt, and baking soda.

In a similar way, priority scheduling would make sure that the most important activities would take place in every phase of the mission. For example, if the computer's memory got overloaded, then the software could automatically pause the least important functions and return to them when enough memory opened up. It sounds obvious, but before this, practically all programs would crash if they had too much to do.

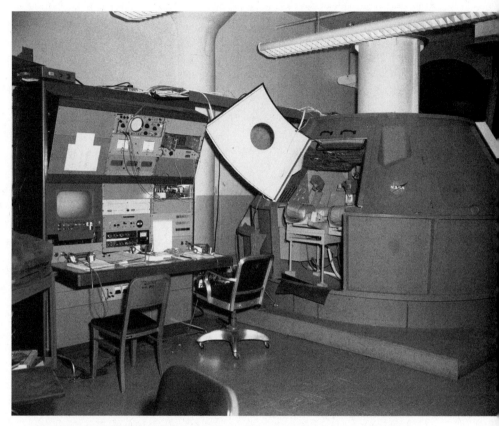

The open hatch leads to the IL's command module simulator, connected to a computer system that simulates a space mission, responding realistically to actions taken by the pilot.

• • •

Margaret's sleepless nights had led her to the amazing insight of error detection and recovery in real time. The key features were priority display together with software restarts and priority scheduling. No longer was the AGC doing only what it was told to do (for example, calculating the position of the spacecraft or firing the main engine in response to a request from the astronaut). Now it was acting like a fourth member of the crew—a troubleshooter who was watching out for the astronauts and taking corrective action when necessary. After this, computer software would never be the same.

KATHERINE JOHNSON

The AGC onboard flight software was filled with equations that could compute practically anything an astronaut needed to know about the motions of the spacecraft. These equations could be quite complex. One of the pioneers writing them for the U.S. manned space program was a modest mathematician at the NASA Langley Research Center in Virginia—Katherine Johnson.

A generation older than Margaret, Johnson started doing calculations for aircraft research before moving to the brand-new field of space-flight. Facing discrimination because she was both Black and a woman, Johnson stood out for her brilliance. In an era before widespread use of electronic computers, she

Katherine Johnson in 1966.

could analyze a problem, write a system of equations to solve it, and then do the intricate calculations herself. When computers were first brought to NASA, she would check their work. Later she developed some of the methods for calculating Apollo trajectories.

On the next page is one of Johnson's equations for the flight-path angle of a spacecraft reentering the atmosphere. The letters stand for different variables and constants, such as the velocity of the vehicle, the altitude above Earth's surface, and the results of previous calcu-

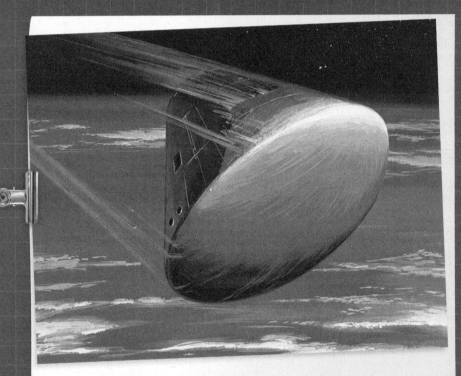

Artist's conception of an Apollo command module reentering the atmosphere. The flight angle is crucial to the survival of the ship and the crew.

lations. Reentry is one of the most dangerous parts of spaceflight. Come in at the wrong angle and the spacecraft could be destroyed. Therefore, Johnson's solutions to this and similar life-or-death problems were crucial.

$$\gamma = \pm \left[\gamma_d^2 + 2K_2B\left(y_d - y\right) - 2\,\frac{g}{V_1^2}\,\Delta h\left(1 - \frac{V_1^2}{gr}\right) \right]^{1/2}$$

Johnson's equation for reentering the atmosphere.

Mariner 1 takes off on July 22, 1962, on the first U.S. mission to target Venus. The rocket soon crashed into the Atlantic Ocean due to a software bug.

CHAPTER 19

THE BUG DETECTIVE

IN J. R. R. TOLKIEN'S FANTASY NOVEL *THE HOBBIT*, EVIL GOB-lins trap the hero and fourteen other members of his party in a grove of trees. There, the demons set fire to the undergrowth and dance around the flames, comparing their captives to hapless birds and singing:

> *Fifteen birds in five firtrees,*
> *their feathers were fanned in a fiery breeze!*
> *But, funny little birds, they had no wings!*
> *O what shall we do with the funny little things?*

In the 1960s, Tolkien's books were especially popular with college students in the Boston area. Inevitably, computer programmers fell in love with them too. The song of the goblins may have inspired Margaret's term for software errors that disrupt a test run and then frustratingly vanish before they can be found and fixed. She called these fleeting bugs "funny little things," or FLTs.

• • •

Software bugs are programming errors that give the wrong answer in a calculation, send the program on a wild goose chase, bring the computer to a screeching halt, or otherwise defeat what the program is supposed to do. When Margaret worked on SAGE, bugs announced themselves like a fire engine driving through the building, with flashing lights and a loud siren signaling that the mammoth XD-1 had failed. Mistakes were hard to miss, and she noted that everyone "would come running to find out whose program crashed. Since it belonged to the programmer standing in front of the console, it was no secret who the guilty one was."

The AGC was far less dramatic in signaling bugs, which could lurk anywhere due to the software's bewildering complexity. Finding them ahead of time was urgent since a computer guiding a spacecraft to the Moon and back could not be allowed to fail under any circumstances.

To aid in bug detection, NASA insisted that MIT consult with John Norton, a programming expert who was obsessed with software bugs. Indeed, he was haunted by them. Norton had been in charge of guidance software for NASA's first mission to Venus in 1962. In July of that year he watched as the gleaming rocket carrying the planetary probe took off in the predawn darkness from Cape Canaveral, Florida. All went well for about four minutes. Then tracking data showed the vehicle mysteriously veering off course, heading for a crash in the busy North Atlantic shipping lanes. The only safe option was to hit the self-destruct switch and end the flight immediately. Already so high that it could barely be seen, the rocket flickered as the explosives went off. Then glowing debris rained from the sky, signaling the tragic end to a mission that was supposed to last for months and send back the first data from the vicinity of another planet.

Investigators traced the problem to a mathematical symbol resembling a hyphen that had been left off one of the guidance equations. Although Norton didn't write the code, he had approved the software version of those equations. His lapse, combined with an antenna problem on the ground, had caused the rocket to go astray. Among spaceflight historians, the blunder came to be called "the most expensive hyphen in history," since it doomed an $18.5 million expedition. It was a lesson in how unforgiving software errors could be. Norton kept a newspaper article about the accident in his wallet, and he became like a character in a novel who has seen a loved one murdered and spends his life trying to track down the killers. He was a man with a mission—find software bugs wherever they lurk—and he earned a reputation as the best bug detective in the business. When NASA needed someone to troubleshoot software errors, they called Norton.

That's how this gloomy, tormented genius ended up looking over the shoulders of IL programmers. Margaret's notorious FLTs might elude him, but he caught many bugs that escaped the IL staff, including potentially major problems such as inconsistent mathematical constants. For example, some programmers estimated the ubiquitous number pi (the ratio of the circumference of a circle to its diameter, which shows up frequently in guidance equations) as the fraction 22/7, while others used the far more accurate decimal approximation, 3.14159265. For purposes of flying to the Moon, Norton insisted on the more precise number.

· · ·

When Norton had debugged a program, MIT coders joked that it had been "Nortonized." His approach even had a fancy name, Auge Kugel, a term already widely used around the IL. When Margaret

The Honeywell 1800 (shown here) and other mainframe computers at the IL were essential for detecting software errors. They were programmed to simulate the AGC and every condition the Apollo spacecraft would encounter. Note the continuous printout of code unfolding onto the floor.

first came to the lab, she had no idea what Auge Kugel meant. "I've got to find out what this is," she thought to herself. "I can't let them know I don't know." But she couldn't track down the meaning and finally had to ask. It turns out that Auge Kugel means "eyeball" in German. The method is simply eyeballing—proofreading. Nothing fancy at all! Norton's technique was to read software as if he were a computer executing instructions, much like reading a musical score and imagining the music. The IL programmers employed Auge Kugel too, among other methods. Usually they were debugging their own code, so they were already familiar with it. By contrast, Norton came to the process cold, and yet he could follow the AGC's "music" in great detail and pick out wrong notes.

Since Margaret used complicated tricks to make her code do more with less, Norton found her software hard to follow. It was as if she were writing a symphony, calling on the horns to play one passage, the violins another, and the woodwinds something else. These different parts are called subroutines in computer jargon. "He respected me for being tricky, and I respected him for figuring it out," she said later.

The program listings for an Apollo mission typically comprised over a hundred thousand lines of code, which were printed and bound in thick books such as the one here.

Sometimes Norton's nitpicking irritated the programmers and other IL staff. One engineer was so annoyed with the bug detective's bloodhound-like resolve to track down even the most trivial errors that he inserted a sly remark into a document destined for review. "Norton needs glasses," he wrote in tiny type. He assumed that Norton wouldn't find the quip for days and would react with self-deprecating amusement when he did.

But NASA's eagle-eyed sleuth spotted it right away and hit the roof. MIT's lighthearted attitude was definitely not NASA's style.

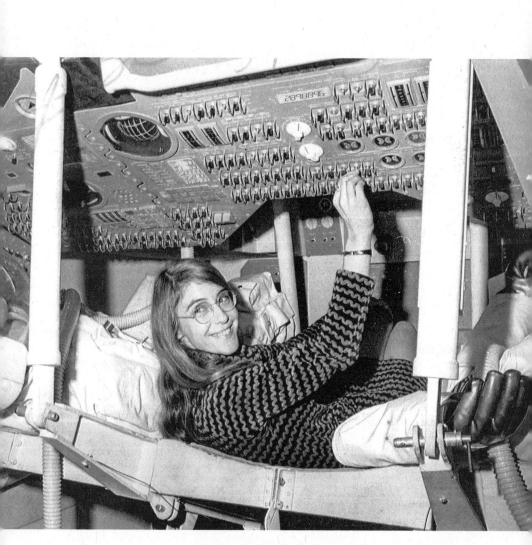

Margaret in the IL's mock-up of the command module.

CHAPTER 20

BLACK FRIDAY

BY 1966, THE CAREFREE ATTITUDE OF IL PROGRAM-
mers was starting to alarm NASA managers. The lab was the only
university-run organization among Apollo's major contractors,
which were mostly large corporations that were accustomed to running complex government projects and meeting tight deadlines. Doc
Draper's close relationship with NASA administrator Jim Webb
had brought the Apollo Guidance Computer contract to MIT in
the first place. Now NASA insiders were starting to have second
thoughts about the Instrumentation Lab's ability to complete the
assignment.

In a way, NASA's complaint was that the IL was too good at
its job. They had designed an onboard computer of unprecedented
reliability and compactness, and now they were in the process of programming it. The trouble was, the computer did not have enough
memory. The IL staff had already figured out how to double the memory and then triple it, but it could not be increased further. Much of
the fault lay with everyone's enthusiasm for the AGC's capabilities.
It was hard to resist adding new features to improve the performance
of the spacecraft and make life easier for the astronauts. And it didn't

help that the astronauts kept insisting on their own changes, which ate up even more memory.

Meeting the schedule was the IL's responsibility, and NASA managers were not optimistic. "There are a number of us who feel that the computer programs for the Apollo spacecraft will soon become the most pacing item for the Apollo flights," concluded NASA troubleshooter Howard W. "Bill" Tindall. By "pacing item," Tindall meant that the software was the lagging item that would determine when Apollo finally flew. Anyone who goes hiking with a group knows that the slowest person should set the pace so that no one is left behind. For the Apollo project, the AGC software was now that slowpoke—not the rocket, the command module, the lunar module, the launch center, or dozens of other complex systems that had to work to meet President Kennedy's goal of landing a man on the Moon by the end of the decade. Those other systems weren't necessarily on schedule either, but the AGC was far behind them.

At a tense gathering at the IL, Tindall put it bluntly: "How can you possibly do this? Here you sit at the very center of the success or failure of this extremely important program. You're behind. Get it through your head you are [fouling] this thing up." Except he used a stronger word than "fouling."

• • •

Tindall's first confrontation with the IL was on Friday, May 13, 1966—Friday the thirteenth, a day that became known around the lab as Black Friday. Other "Black Fridays" followed as Tindall and the IL staff wrestled with getting the AGC software under control. The number-one priority was streamlining the programs—throwing out any that were not absolutely necessary so that the code could fit into the computer's restricted memory. Tindall called these expendable programs "frosting on the cake," and he presided over meeting after meeting where they were summarily scrapped. He also insisted on a 15 percent buffer. In other words, 15 percent of the total memory should always be available just in case.

Bill Tindall confers with NASA controllers.

In short order, gone were many of the IL's cleverest ideas, such as computer control over routine spacecraft maneuvers. Now the astronauts would have to do this manually at the risk of wasting precious maneuvering fuel. Also gone were backup features, such as the AGC's ability to guide the Saturn V—the Moon rocket—during its launch from Florida, in case the rocket's own computer failed.

Margaret barely noticed these deletions, since she was focused on making sure the contributions of hundreds of programmers worked together smoothly, without bugs. However, Tindall's call to keep new code to a minimum did torpedo one of her "what if" ideas, inspired by young Lauren. Now a grade-schooler, Lauren liked to play astronaut when she was visiting her mother at the lab. "She saw me playing that way in simulations we would run," Margaret reminisced. During one such exercise, Lauren "started hitting keys" on the DSKY. "All of a sudden, the simulation started. Then she pressed other keys and the simulation crashed."

Children have a knack for finding fatal flaws. What Lauren had stumbled on was a simple combination of keystrokes that made the software think a Moon-bound spacecraft was actually back on Earth, sitting on the launchpad. An astronaut who made this mistake during a flight would cause the spacecraft to lose its orientation in space, jeopardizing the mission. At a subsequent meeting with NASA and IL managers, Margaret explained what had happened and suggested she write a short piece of code to prevent the "Lauren bug."

"She was just a kid playing around," they replied. "Astronauts don't make mistakes."

"But what if it *does* happen?" Margaret countered.

"Impossible!"

Nonetheless, they did let her write an official note for the mission documents that said, "Do not select P01 during flight," which was the mistake that Lauren had made. Everyone considered it a warning on the order of "Open mouth before inserting food."

When the astronauts read the note, they probably laughed.

"We would never do that!"

· · ·

It was around this time that Margaret started using the term "software engineering" to describe what she and the other programmers were doing. The expression sounded high-flown to the hardware engineers who had created the AGC. Their profession extended back thousands of years to the bridges, pyramids, temples, and other structures of the ancient world. When Dick Battin took charge of the AGC and its software, his wife understood that software was an important technical part of the project. But like most people at the time she had no idea what it was. It sounded so much like soft furnishings— pillows, mattresses, and the like—that she begged her husband not to tell their friends. It didn't fit the engineer's proud self-image.

If nothing else, Bill Tindall's ordeal of Black Fridays had proved that software was a make-or-break aspect of the entire Apollo effort. And what better term for the craft of causing those cryptic instructions to perform miracles of navigation and control than "engineering." Margaret campaigned for this new sign of respect. "It was an ongoing joke for a long time," she observed. "They liked to kid me about my radical ideas."

But eventually this radical idea prevailed. "It was a memorable day when one of the most respected hardware gurus explained to everyone in a meeting that he agreed with me that the process of building software should be considered a formal engineering discipline, just as with hardware."

Apollo 1 crew patch.

CHAPTER 21

THE FIRE

BY EARLY 1967, THE IL HAD RESTORED ITS GOOD standing with NASA. In a memo on January 23, Bill Tindall said he expected the latest batch of software "to perform very well for us." Lightheartedly, he added, "I don't know why I'm sticking my neck out on a prediction like that. Just living dangerously, I guess." His combative tone had all but vanished, and he and the IL staff were working as a team.

The other pieces of Apollo were also falling into place. A series of two-person, Earth-orbiting missions called Gemini had just ended, giving astronauts crucial piloting experience in space. Robotic probes had landed on the Moon and also circled it, investigating potential Apollo landing sites. The lunar module and the Saturn V were due for separate unmanned tests later in the year. And Apollo 1, the first crewed flight of the command module, a two-week shakedown mission in Earth orbit, was expected to launch in late February.

With fingers crossed, NASA officials were looking forward to putting humans on the Moon sometime in 1968, a full year before President Kennedy's deadline.

Tragically, this dream soon went up in smoke.

On January 27, 1967, four days after Tindall's upbeat memo, astronauts Gus Grissom, Ed White, and Roger Chaffee were sealed in their Apollo 1 command module on the launchpad in Florida, participating in a countdown dress rehearsal. A stray spark from an electrical short circuit ignited a fire inside their spacecraft. Unable to escape quickly, the astronauts never had a chance. All three died in a matter of seconds from breathing toxic gasses produced by the blaze.

The Apollo 1 astronauts and their backup crew (all sitting) pose with IL engineers (standing). Gus Grissom and Roger Chaffee are at the far left, and Ed White is at the far right. They were to make the Apollo 1 flight until tragedy struck.

News of the tragedy spread rapidly. At the IL, workers were mostly on a dinner break or gone for the day. But engineer Hugh Blair-Smith happened to be at the lab. After absorbing the horror of the event, he began to wonder, "Will this be the end of Apollo?" Obviously, an investigation would follow, but the death of three astronauts in a state-of-the-art CM in a supposedly safe ground test suggested that the complex Apollo effort might be harboring hidden flaws.

NASA put Apollo on hold for several months and conducted a comprehensive review, focusing on the cause of the accident but also seeking out trouble spots in other areas. Defective wiring and flammable materials, combined with high-pressure oxygen in the cabin, turned out to be the culprit in the fire. The CM was upgraded to fix these problems, and the hatch was redesigned so it could be opened in a hurry. That was just the beginning. Altogether, some five thousand changes—large and small—were made in the CM. Meanwhile, Apollo managers working on other parts of the project had a chance to step back, identify issues that needed correcting, make the necessary changes, and instill a renewed commitment to perfection in their workers. The delay also provided breathing room to catch up with the schedule.

At the IL, Blair-Smith noted that a software review revealed "a disturbing number of flaws that could have created embarrassing problems in Apollo 1 if it had flown." These weren't necessarily life-threatening, he wrote, but they could easily have ended the mission early. They got fixed.

• • •

Putting Apollo back on track after the fire took most of 1967. The turning point came in early November with the first launch of the Saturn V. Taller than the Statue of Liberty and weighing more than six million pounds, the rocket worked almost flawlessly, sending a command module into Earth orbit and then simulating a high-speed return from the Moon. Of all the Apollo components that *had* to work, the Saturn V was paramount, since it was impossible to get the heavy Apollo spacecraft to the Moon and back without it.

The first flight of the Saturn V Moon rocket sent an unmanned command module, guided by an AGC, into deep space for a high-speed return to Earth. Here the spacecraft is fished from the ocean, showing charring from its plunge through the atmosphere.

Aboard the CM for this mission was an early version of the AGC, programmed to control the module's propulsion system and guide the ship to a precise reentry and splashdown in the Pacific Ocean. Since there were no astronauts on the flight, nor a lunar module, the software was comparatively simple.

Meanwhile, the far more complex programs for future missions were in the works, and Margaret was managing the teams of specialists who were writing them.

Kenneth Heafield, Professor of
English at Delta College, 1967.

CHAPTER 22

KENNETH

A YEAR OR TWO AFTER SHE STARTED AT THE Instrumentation Lab, Margaret traveled back to Michigan to visit her parents and siblings and their families. It was Christmastime, and people were gathered in the living room of her parents' house. Someone asked what she was working on. She described how she was writing the software that astronauts would use for a trip to the Moon. They looked at her wide-eyed. A moment later when she left the room their eyes rolled, as if to say, "What is Margaret up to now?!" No one knew what software was, and the Apollo program, although it was in the news, seemed like a project that would never happen.

But Margaret's father, Kenneth, had a different attitude. He didn't understand software either, but he understood Margaret. Ever since she was in college he had felt that her interest in abstract mathematics had a lot in common with his passion for poetry and philosophy. Each of these fields deals with ideas. Her work demanded intense thought, and so did writing a poem or constructing a philosophical argument. If she was part of the effort to send humans to the Moon, then he was sure her diligence would help make it happen.

For years, Kenneth had crafted beautiful poems and sent them to small periodicals. By 1964, he had enough for a small pamphlet, which he published and dedicated to Margaret. She was touched. "It was the best thing anyone ever did for me," she later said.

He did other writing too, including a routine job for a publisher of professional books that wanted him to draft a manual for legal secretaries in collaboration with an expert in the field. The result, *Principles and Practices for the Legal Secretary*, is the most eloquent book ever written on the subject, full of good advice for running a law office and for life in general. "Is it possible to be accurate all of the time?" the book asks in a discussion much like those Kenneth used to have with Margaret when she was young. "Of course it is," the text continues. "Ask the gardener tending his flower bed why his garden has no weeds among the roses. Silly question, he'll say. He knows the weeds from the flowers, and he pulls the weeds. It is as simple as that . . . If errors are detected and eliminated as you work, the finished product will be perfect." In her coding for the AGC, Margaret understood this lesson very well.

The book is surely the only secretarial manual that quotes the poets John Keats, John Donne, and Shakespeare, along with Abraham Lincoln, Benjamin Franklin, and Michelangelo. The last chapter sums up the book with a surprisingly moving scene, featuring a young legal secretary named Suzanne. She has been on the job for a year and is preparing to close the office at the end of a winter day after everyone else has left. Noticing that it has started snowing outside, she decides to wait out the storm before heading home. Alone as the snow collects on the window ledge, she reflects on her experiences of the preceding months. She has learned the rudiments of her profession, but she has discovered so much more—the wisdom of clients, the duty to think, the rewards of working on a team, and how to make her job a labor of love.

After the snow in Detroit, Michigan.

As the storm passes and Suzanne departs into the beautiful wintry calm, the book quotes the Lebanese American poet Kahlil Gibran: "If you cannot work with love but only with distaste, it is better that you should leave your work and sit at the gate of the temple and take alms of those who work with joy."

The publisher had given Kenneth the seemingly tedious assignment to coauthor a textbook for legal secretaries. He had made it into something magical—an artful guide on how to live.

• • •

Kenneth visited Margaret in Cambridge in the fall of 1967, as NASA was recovering from the Apollo 1 fire. At the time, he was an administrator and professor of English at Delta College in Michigan, where he was the beloved campus poet. The *Detroit News* called him "one of the few mortals who inhabit the nation's college campuses as resident poets . . . [thinking] big thoughts about the meaning of life." Appropriately, he was also president of the Poetry Society of Michigan.

Margaret noticed he had a cold during his visit, but she didn't think anything of it. She didn't realize he was having heart problems. By the time he drove back to Michigan, his cold had turned into pneumonia. He checked into a hospital, and soon after he died of a heart attack. He was only fifty-seven years old. When Margaret came out for the funeral she discovered he had a shelf full of books on the heart. He had known he was ill but kept it to himself.

Kenneth Heafield, 1960s.

Kenneth in the courtyard of Delta College, spring 1967.

In its profile of Kenneth, the *Detroit News* caught a glimpse of a man thinking confidently about the future: "Florid, with greying crew cut and pale blue eyes, the poet talks about civilization as if it were just about to flower into something significant." But death too was clearly on his mind, as the last verse from his poem "Curfew" hints:

> *Good night*
> *All that I know.*
> *The greater and lesser light*
> *Will come and go.*
> *All this, and more,*
> *I know. And so*
> *Good night.*

When his hometown paper interviewed family members for an obituary, the reporter misheard "poetry" as "poultry," and credited Kenneth with being president of the State Poultry Society of Michigan. He would have had a good laugh over that.

The Moon up close,
mostly showing the side
never seen from Earth.

PART 3

TO THE MOON

The view from lunar orbit, photographed by Apollo 8 astronauts. The largest crater in the image, partially cut off at the left, is about 70 miles across.

CHAPTER 23

APOLLO 8

ASTRONAUT JIM LOVELL FLOATED DOWN TO THE command module's lower equipment bay, which was the cubby beneath the row of three seats where Lovell and his comrades, Frank Borman and Bill Anders, had just ridden a Saturn V into Earth orbit. It was December 21, 1968, and this was the Apollo 8 mission, the flight that would give the Apollo Guidance Computer and its software the most crucial test yet. Could the unit guide the spacecraft to the Moon, into lunar orbit, and then back home? No humans had ever gone farther than a few hundred miles above Earth. Now three were venturing to the Moon, 240,000 miles away. There would be no landing attempt on this outing since the lunar module was not yet ready.

In the lower equipment bay, Lovell steadied himself next to the telescope and sextant, which were mounted in the side of the ship. He flipped a switch ejecting the optics cover into space, peered through an eyepiece, and found two stars, including Sirius, the brightest star in the sky. Centering each star in the field of view, he pushed a button, sending a signal to the computer. Since launch, the software had been keeping track of the spacecraft's changing position. The AGC compared the new star sightings with where it thought the stars should be. Then it updated the coordinates, giving a new fix on the ship's exact location in the universe. The process was called realigning the inertial platform, and Lovell would do it many times during the mission, since the inertial measurement unit tended to drift off course.

The next step was to leave low Earth orbit. After a countdown, the remaining top stage of the Saturn reignited, accelerating the Apollo spacecraft to near escape velocity, the speed needed to break free of Earth's gravitational tug. The software monitored the burn, which lasted five minutes and seventeen seconds and went perfectly. Apollo 8 was now on its way to the Moon. It would be a three-day trip.

Meanwhile in the SCAMA room at MIT, Dick Battin, who had been working on the Apollo project for seven years, couldn't believe a lunar voyage was finally underway. "I turned to the guy next to me and said, 'My God, they're really going to do this!'"

• • •

Margaret was also in the SCAMA room. It had been a year since her father's death. During that time she had been frantically busy helping manage a team of over four hundred specialists who were writing software for Apollo 8 and the other missions that would lead to a lunar landing, expected to take place on either Apollo 10, 11, 12, or 13. It was hard to say which mission it would be, since so much about the Apollo effort was unproven, including the AGC.

For the duration of the Apollo 8 flight, IL team members staffed the SCAMA room around the clock so they could deal with any computer emergencies that came up. For most of the six-day mission, none did.

Margaret and three colleagues in the
SCAMA room during Apollo 8.

Days one, two, and three were devoted to Lovell's navigation sightings and platform alignments. He was like a nervous hiker, obsessively consulting his map and compass to make sure he knew exactly where he was. NASA wanted to prove that if radar contact from Earth was lost, the astronauts could find their way back home. In the meantime, Borman conducted two midcourse corrections to ensure their ship would come close to the Moon without hitting it. One of Anders's jobs was to take pictures of the shrinking Earth out the window. Except for his photography, all these activities involved the AGC.

At the end of day three, they hurtled within eighty-seven miles of the Moon, as lunar gravity pulled them around like a race car rounding a curve. The astronauts instructed the computer to fire their main engine, slowing the spacecraft just enough to be captured into lunar orbit. This tricky maneuver took place on December 24, Christmas Eve. Since the rocket burn happened on the far side of the Moon, out of contact with Earth, no one on the ground knew whether it had succeeded until the spacecraft emerged from the other side. When it finally did, the crew reported they had attained a near-perfect orbit, which was a pleasant surprise, given all the unknowns. The packed SCAMA room erupted in cheers.

The Christmas Eve timing was pure coincidence, having to do with the phase of the Moon and other factors. Observing the holiday

While in lunar orbit, the Apollo 8 astronauts famously photographed Earthrise.

with an unforgettable broadcast, Borman, Lovell, and Anders read from the book of Genesis in a live TV transmission from lunar orbit. The next day, Christmas, they received a welcome gift when their rocket relit on computer command, boosting them out of lunar orbit and on a three-day journey back to Earth.

The return trajectory had to be even more precise than the trip out since the reentry window into Earth's atmosphere is very narrow. Come in too steeply, and the ship will slow down so fast that the crew will be killed by the braking force or else incinerated like a meteor by frictional heating. Come in too shallow, and the spacecraft will stay in space, circling Earth in long elliptical orbits, with no second chance for the astronauts to return home before their oxygen runs out.

The Apollo 8 crew claimed they never thought about all the horrible ways they could die in space, which was probably true; they were too busy to let their minds wander. A member of the Apollo 11 crew would describe how a mission to the Moon is a fragile daisy chain of events, each of which has to go perfectly. The focus of the crew and controllers is always on the next sequence of steps. It's like being in the middle of a hard-fought football game, in which total concentration is on the play being run at that particular moment. Margaret and her colleagues in the SCAMA room shared this intense focus on whatever was happening right then.

• • •

The SCAMA room was quiet in the early evening hours of Christmas, which was the fifth day of the mission. Margaret and a handful of others were sitting around in case any problems came up. The crew had recently performed a midcourse correction to perfect their trajectory back to Earth. Lovell was now in the middle of one of his star sightings. He had gotten so good at it that he later joked he was like a virtuoso pianist, playing the computer's DSKY as if it were a grand

Aboard Apollo 8, Jim Lovell takes one of countless star sightings.

piano. He was fast too. But at this moment he was also very tired, having had little sleep since launch.

"Oops!" he said half aloud. Anders, who was on watch while Borman slept, overheard. At the same moment, Anders noticed that the instrument showing the spacecraft's orientation started to move, indicating an unplanned maneuver. In fact, the ship wasn't doing anything unusual; the instrument had simply reset to its reading on the launchpad.

Meanwhile, on the computer the essential navigation data that would tell the crew how to get home had vanished.

Lauren and Margaret.

CHAPTER 24

THE LAUREN BUG

ANYONE WHO HAS EVER BROKEN AN EXPENSIVE object, caused an accident, or watched helplessly as a treasured possession falls overboard into deep water knows the feeling that Jim Lovell had when he hit the wrong keys on the DSKY and saw his painstakingly compiled navigation data disappear.

Lovell radioed Mission Control in Houston: "For some reason, we suddenly got a Program 01 and no attitude light on our computer." He didn't realize it at first, but instead of entering "Star 01" he had entered "Program 01." This told the software that the spacecraft was back on the launchpad. In the process, it erased information on the craft's current location and orientation—or attitude—and quite possibly corrupted other data.

• • •

At the SCAMA room, Margaret immediately knew what had happened. "Guess what?" she said to her teammates. "It's the Lauren bug!" It was the error that Lauren had caused months earlier when she was playing astronaut on the simulator. Margaret had wanted to fix it then but was told, "Astronauts don't make mistakes." Now Lovell, one of the most experienced astronauts, had made that very blunder. NASA was promptly on the line to the Instrumentation Lab, trying to gauge the seriousness of the situation.

The SCAMA room during Apollo 8. Margaret is at the table, which is piled with documents, charts, program listings, and the case for a slide rule for performing quick calculations (see page 188). Mission events are written on two chalkboards.

Lovell's next step was obvious. He had to realign the inertial measurement unit, telling the computer where the ship was in space and which way was up, down, left, and right. This meant taking several star sightings. Normally, he would enter the number for a star, such as Polaris in the handle of the Little Dipper. The software would then steer the navigation optics to the star's predicted location, and he would check for any discrepancies. However, now the software had no idea where the stars were. Lovell had to search the tiny field of view through the telescope, confused by ice crystals surrounding the spacecraft, which sparkled like stars. Even so, he was confident he could get a reasonably accurate navigation fix. What worried him, the crew, Mission Control, and MIT was that the Lauren bug might have caused unforeseen problems deep inside the computer. Bugs could do that.

Borman had been awakened by the incident and got on the radio: "Is there any danger that this might have screwed up any other part of memory that would be involved with entry or anything like that?"

Houston assured him that they didn't think so. In fact, they didn't know. Borman was the mission commander, and they wanted him to go back to sleep since he was as tired as the others. In the meantime MIT, Lovell, and Anders worked on a solution.

Mission Control in Houston during Apollo 8. The crew that will fly on Apollo 11 are all present: Mike Collins at far left, and Neil Armstrong (sitting) and Buzz Aldrin (standing), both wearing dark jackets.

• • •

About two hours after the mishap, Mission Control requested a "memory dump," meaning a record of the entire contents of the AGC's erasable memory. Soon after, Lovell transmitted the data to Earth. Then Margaret and her colleagues began poring over the code—made up of temporary programs, calculations in progress, and other fleeting data—looking for any problems caused by the Lauren bug. "We were going through the program listings faster than I've ever gone through a listing in my life," Margaret later said. Her team was using the Auge Kugel method, just like John Norton, eyeballing the code and "pretending we were the computer," reasoning through each line of instructions. They did this for the next seven hours. Finally, Mission Control radioed good news to the crew: "It looks like it's all okay."

A little over thirty hours later, Apollo 8 made a perfect reentry and splashdown.

• • •

As soon as the crisis was over, NASA asked Margaret to go ahead and write the short program she had recommended after the original Lauren incident. It didn't take long, and the code said essentially: "If the astronaut keys in Program 01 at any time other than prelaunch, then don't do it!"

Lovell himself would later command a truly harrowing flight, Apollo 13. That mission was outbound to the Moon in April 1970, when an oxygen tank behind the command module ruptured. With life-supporting supplies dwindling away, the crippled ship had to

Borman, Lovell, and Anders at the end of Apollo 8's six-day voyage to the Moon.

make a four-day emergency return to Earth. Despite this epic ordeal, which became the subject of books, movies, and TV documentaries, Lovell reportedly said that his most frightening moment of all in spaceflight was the Lauren bug on Apollo 8.

THE OTHER ONBOARD COMPUTER

In the "be prepared" spirit of Boy Scouts, astronauts were ready in case the AGC went out and they also lost contact with Mission Control. During spaceflights, they carried charts and tables with vital navigation data. But suppose they had to solve an equation like the one on page 145? With pencil, paper, values for constants, and an ingenious device called a slide rule, they could quickly estimate an answer.

Invented in the 1600s, slide rules were widely used by engineers and scientists until the invention of battery-powered pocket calculators in the 1970s. Requiring no electricity, the ruler-like devices combined different mathematical scales that allowed the user to multiply, divide, and perform other operations with the aid of a sliding central strip and an adjustable indicator. Everything was controlled by hand.

Of course, what *can* happen in space eventually *will* happen. In a mission preceding Apollo, astronauts Jim Lovell and Buzz Aldrin lost their radar on a two-person Gemini flight in November 1966, greatly reducing the effectiveness of their primitive onboard computer. They were more than seventy miles from the unmanned Agena spacecraft

View out Aldrin's window as the Gemini 12 spacecraft closes in on the Agena target vehicle.

they wanted to intercept in a test of the rendezvous and docking procedure for the lunar and command modules. Using a sextant, a slide rule, and charts to calculate their range and closing rate, and feeding these numbers into the onboard computer, Aldrin painstakingly determined the maneuvers needed to reach the target—which they did with great efficiency in about an hour.

Aldrin also relied on what he called his "Mark One Cranium Computer"—his brain. "I pretty much had to calculate the coordinates in my head with the help of my Picket slide rule that I had brought along just in case," he later explained.

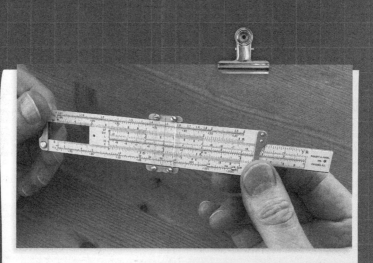

A Picket slide rule like the one used on Gemini 12 and later carried on Apollo flights.

After the Apollo program, handheld electronic calculators replaced slide rules, but veteran users of the "slipstick," as the slide rule was nicknamed, liked to race operators of the new calculators in getting answers to problems—especially long strings of calculations. The slipstick champions usually won.

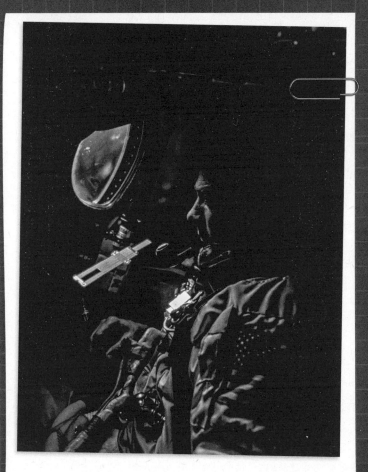

A slide rule floats in front of Buzz Aldrin during the Gemini 12 mission in 1966.

Piloted by Armstrong and Aldrin, the Apollo 11 lunar module heads down to the Moon.

CHAPTER 25

APOLLO 11

APOLLO 8 THRILLED IL PROGRAMMERS AS THEY watched their software perform flawlessly on the first trip by astronauts to the Moon and back. For many in the space program, Apollo 8 was the high point of the entire man-on-the-Moon effort, since it involved an unprecedented number of new procedures and unknown perils. The experience was also nerve-racking beyond belief for anyone who had even a minor part in the mission, and also for the hundreds of millions who followed it in the news. But President Kennedy's goal was to *land* on the Moon, not just orbit it. This required a lunar module, and the LM had its own Apollo Guidance Computer, with programs designed to manage the risky descent to the surface and the ascent back to the orbiting command module.

By this point, Margaret was in charge of all onboard flight software, meaning she was responsible for every program used by astronauts on a lunar mission. Hundreds of people were contributing to these programs, and she was the captain of the ship, tasked with making it all work. Appropriately, her salary was doubled. "When I took over," she later observed, "one of the bosses at the top said he had no doubt I could do the job but was worried the men working in the group might rebel. Well, they didn't. More than anything, we were dedicated to the missions and worked side by side to solve the challenging problems and to meet the critical deadlines."

NASA used the next two flights to perfect different phases of a landing mission. Apollo 9, which flew in March 1969, tested the CM and LM in low Earth orbit. Launched two months later, Apollo 10 flew all the way to the Moon and into lunar orbit, just like Apollo 8, but this time with a LM attached. The two ships separated, and the LM descended to within nine and a half miles of the lunar surface before rejoining the command module. Apollo 10 was a dress rehearsal for the next flight, Apollo 11, which would be the first to attempt a landing. Few thought Apollo 11 would succeed, since landing was the most difficult part of a complete Apollo mission, requiring the AGC to process data close to its limit. The likeliest outcome was that something would go wrong and that the mission would be cut short, returning to Earth for another try on a later flight.

Apollo 11 was set for July—just five months short of President Kennedy's goal of putting a man on the Moon "before this decade is out."

• • •

Apollo 11 was to be commanded by Neil Armstrong, the astronaut who had earlier caught the eye of an IL engineer who was very impressed by "the questions he asked and how well prepared and thoughtful" he was. Scheduled to accompany Armstrong to the lunar surface was Buzz Aldrin, who had earned a doctorate in astronautics from MIT. His thesis was on orbital rendezvous, the maneuver that would bring the LM and CM back together after the Moon walk. He was so expert in the procedure that other astronauts called him "Dr. Rendezvous."

Assigned to pilot the CM was Mike Collins, a test pilot with an unusual taste for poetry, particularly the English poet John Milton, whose verse returns again and again to the image of that "resplendent globe," the Moon. In the 1630s, Milton visited Galileo Galilei, the scientist who revolutionized astronomy by turning a new invention called the telescope on the Moon and other celestial bodies. Margaret's father would have loved talking to Collins, who believed that fluency with words was just as important to technical projects as math, science, and engineering—and that good poetry was language at its most fluent.

• • •

The Apollo Guidance Computer was ingeniously constructed to be hardy, small, and powerful. It had a fixed memory literally woven into place with thin copper wires strung around and through tiny donut-shaped magnetic cores. A wire passing through a core represented a one in the computer's binary language; an empty core was a zero. A completed AGC had three miles of wire and just over three thousand cores. Along with erasable memory for temporary data, as well as other electronic components, the entire unit filled a package measuring one square foot and weighing just seventy pounds.

In a plant about twenty miles from MIT, teams of women with superb manual dexterity threaded copper wires in and out among the cores, translating the IL's program listings into physical circuitry. Such precise work was a tradition in this part of Massachusetts, which

The AGC's fixed memory was wired by dexterous hands, mostly female.

was a center for fine watchmaking and weaving going back more than a century.

The flight software for every Apollo mission was different, sometimes markedly so. Each AGC was tailor-made in a manufacturing process that took about two months. Given time for testing and installation, the program listings had to be "frozen" with no further changes three to four months before the mission flew. Margaret signed off on Apollo 11's command module software on March 28, and she approved the lunar module's program package around the same time. Three and a half months later, Apollo 11 was ready for takeoff.

• • •

Before the flight, MIT sent a photographer to the Instrumentation Lab for publicity pictures. This was easy for the AGC hardware since the photographer could pose an engineer next to AGC components or indeed any complicated-looking piece of equipment in the lab. Newspaper readers would expect such images and be duly impressed. But software was another story.

"We have to get some pictures of the software," the photographer told Margaret. "How in the world do you take a picture of software?" he muttered. "You can't see it."

But in Margaret's office, he noticed volume after volume of bound computer printouts. These, she explained, were the listings for the AGC software: every line of code in the core and erasable memory—and not just for Apollo 11, but for earlier missions and future

```
GAP: ASSEMBLE REVISION 055 OF AGC PROGRAM COMANCHE BY NASA 2021113-051      10:25 APR. 1,1969    (MAIN)    PAGE    1
L        ASSEMBLY AND OPERATION INFORMATION                                  USER'S PAGE NO.    1        EO
R000001
R000002  *************************************************************************
R000003  *                                                                       *
R000004  *        THIS AGC PROGRAM SHALL ALSO BE REFERRED TO AS:                  *
R000005  *                                                                       *
R000006  *                                                                       *
R000007  *                        COLOSSUS 2A                                    *
R000008  *                                                                       *
R000009  *                                                                       *
R000010  *        THIS PROGRAM IS INTENDED FOR USE IN THE CM AS SPECIFIED         *
R000011  *        IN REPORT R-577. THIS PROGRAM WAS PREPARED UNDER DSR            *
R000012  *        PROJECT 55-23870, SPONSORED BY THE MANNED SPACECRAFT            *
R000013  *        CENTER OF THE NATIONAL AERONAUTICS AND SPACE                    *
R000014  *        ADMINISTRATION THROUGH CONTRACT NAS 9-4065 WITH THE             *
R000015  *        INSTRUMENTATION LABORATORY, MASSACHUSETTS INSTITUTE OF          *
R000016  *        TECHNOLOGY, CAMBRIDGE, MASS.                                    *
R000017  *                                                                       *
R000018  *************************************************************************
R000019           SUBMITTED:  MARGARET H. HAMILTON           DATE:  28 MAR 69
R00002            M.H.HAMILTON, COLOSSUS PROGRAMMING LEADER
R000021           APOLLO GUIDANCE AND NAVIGATION
R000022           APPROVED:   DANIEL J. LICKLY               DATE:  28 MAR 69
R000023           D.J.LICKLY, DIRECTOR, MISSION PROGRAM DEVELOPMENT
R000024           APOLLO GUIDANCE AND NAVIGATION PROGRAM
R000025           APPROVED: FRED H. MARTIN                   DATE:  28 MAR 69
R000026           FRED H. MARTIN, COLOSSUS PROJECT MANGER
R000027           APOLLO GUIDANCE AND NAVIGATION PROGRAM
R000028           APPROVED: NORMAN E.SEARS                   DATE:  28 MAR 69
R000029           N.E. SEARS, DIRECTOR, MISSION DEVELOPMENT
R00003            APOLLO GUIDANCE AND NAVIGATION PROGRAM
R000031           APPROVED: RICHARD H. BATTIN                DATE:  28 MAR 69
R000032           R.H. BATTIN, DIRECTOR, MISSION DEVELOPMENT
R000033           APOLLO GUIDANCE AND NAVIGATION PROGRAM
R000034           APPROVED: DAVID G. HOAG                    DATE:  28 MAR 69
R000035           D.G. HOAG, DIRECTOR
R000036           APOLLO GUIDANCE AND NAVIGATION PROGRAM
R000037
R000038           APPROVED: RALPH R. RAGAN                   DATE:  28 MAR 69
R000039           R.R. RAGAN, DEPUTY DIRECTOR
R00004            INSTRUMENTATION LABORATORY
R000041
```

Page 1 of the 1,751-page printout of the computer code for the Apollo 11 command module, submitted by Margaret.

missions. *This* was the software, she said, millions of lines of it. They decided to make a stack of the listings as tall as Margaret—five feet, four inches. "I was laughing during the photo session because I was afraid the stack was going to fall on me," she vividly remembered. (See the photo on p. vi, opposite the contents page.)

• • •

For those involved in Project Apollo, so much was going on and the missions were so tightly spaced in late 1968 and 1969—scheduled at roughly two-month intervals—that there was no special drama connected to Apollo 11. It was *all* drama *all* the time. In Margaret's case, no sooner had she signed off on Apollo 11's software than she plunged into the requirements for the next mission, and the mission after that. Her routine changed the moment a mission was off the ground. That was the starting gun for the latest real-time test of the AGC and its onboard flight software against everything the system was being asked to do. Around the IL, the attitude was almost, "What mission is this? Oh, yeah, Apollo 11, the one that's supposed to land on the Moon."

• • •

Apollo 11 launched on July 16. Three days later, the astronauts were orbiting the Moon. Neil and Buzz floated into the LM, checked the systems, and undocked, leaving Mike Collins behind in the CM. After another half orbit, Neil instructed the AGC to fire the descent rocket to slow their speed and send the LM on a controlled plunge toward the lunar surface. The software had to track the LM's speed, position, altitude, fuel, and other changing values, while also standing

Armstrong (left) and Aldrin train for Apollo 11 in a lunar module simulator. The DSKY is between them.

by to rocket the crew back to the CM in case of an emergency. The astronauts were among the world's best pilots, but there was no way they could land the LM without the AGC's help.

Everything was going well, but then five minutes after firing the descent rocket, Armstrong made an unexpected call to Mission Control.

"Program alarm . . . It's a 1202," he said, giving the code number on the LM's display screen, where a warning light indicated trouble.

At the SCAMA room, Margaret looked over at Fred Martin, one of the project managers. They both had expressions that said, "This isn't supposed to happen!"

APPLICABLE TO: IN DESCENT, AVERAGE-G ON

ALARM CODE	TYPE	PRE-MANUAL CAPABILITY	MANUAL CAPABILITY
00105 MK ROUT. BUSY	POODOO	* * * PGNCS GUID. LOST, * * *PGNCS/AGS ABRT/ABRT STG * (decision how on current rules) * (NO LR DATA)	PGNCS GUIDANCE NO/GO (PGNCS GO for TAPE METERS, CROSS-POINTERS, CONTROL, ABORTING) (NO LR DATA)
00430 CANT INTG. SV.	"		
01103 CCSHOLE-PROG. BUG	"		
01204 NEG. WAITLIST	"		
01206 DSKY, TWO USERS	"		
01302 NEG. SQ. ROOT	"		
01501 DSKY, PROG. BAD	"		
01502 DSKY, PROG. BUG	"		
00607 LRHB, NO SOLN	"		
"O.F." = Overflow, too many. CONTINUING ← OCCURRENCE OF:		DUTY CYCLE MAY DEGRADE PGNCS (AGS CONTROL MAY HELP- SEE BELOW) (WATCH FOR OTHER CUES) PGNCS CONDITION UNKNOWN DSKY MAY BE LOCKED UP DUTY CYCLE MAY BE UP TO POINT OF MISSING SOME FUNCTIONS (NAV. LAST TO DIE) SWITCH TO AGS (FOLLOW ERR NEEDLES) MAY HELP (REDUCES PGNCS DUTY CYCLE SIGNIF.)	SAME AS LEFT (except "other cues" which would otherwise be cause for ABORT PROBABLY AREN'T, INSTEAD IT WOULD BE PGNCS GUIDANCE NO/GO - COMPLETE MANUAL LANDING IN AGS.)
01104 DELAY ROUT. O.V.	BAILOUT		
01201 EXECT. O.F. (VAC)	"		
01202 EXECT. O.F. (JOBS)	"		
01203 EXECT. O.F.(TASKS)	"		
01207 EXECT. O.F. (HRKS)	"		
01210 TWO USERS	"		
01211 MRK ROUT. INTRPT	"		
02000 DAP O.F.	"		
ISS WARNING WITH:		PIPA/CDU/IMU FAIL DISCRETES PRESENT (Other mission rules suffice; alarm may help point to what rule will be broken)	same as left
00777 PIPA FAIL	LIGHT ONLY		
03777 CDU FAIL	"		
09777 PIPA, CDU FAIL	"		
07777 IMU FAIL	"		
10777 PIPA, IMU FAIL	"		
13777 CDU, IMU FAIL	"		
14777 PIPA, CDU, IMU FL	"		
00214 IMU TURNED OFF	LIGHT ONLY	* * AGS ABRT/ABRT STAGE * * *	SWITCH TO AGS PGNS NO/GO on Gand C (poss. NO/GO on NAV.)
01107 E-Mem. Destroyed	FRESH STRT	* AGS ABRT/ABRT STAGE * * *	SWITCH TO AGS PGNCS NO/GO! (IMU as ref. okay)
CONTINUING ← 00402 BAD GUID. CMDS	LIGHT ONLY	*IF ALARM DOESN'T STOP: *same as "POODO's" (ABRT?)	If ALARM DOESN'T STOP: Same as "POODO's"
CONTINUING ← 01406 GUID. NO SOLN 01410 GUID O.V.	LIGHT ONLY	PGNCS GUID, NO/GO AS LONG AS ALARM OCCURRING (ATT. HOLD, CONST. GTC, CONT. OK) (ABRT WILL PROB. COME FROM CURRENT RULES e.g. GTC vs. V.) WATCH GTC ←	same as left (except prob. no abort.)

Jack Garman's cheat sheet of alarm codes. When 1202 flashed, he scanned down the list to the third line in the second set of rows. His notes told him to "watch for other cues." These might "be cause for abort." "Probably aren't," he had added.

CHAPTER 26

NEVER-SUPPOSED-TO-HAPPEN ALARMS

MARGARET AND HER COLLEAGUES USED THE expression "never-supposed-to-happen alarms" for situations that were especially worrisome and rare. The 1202 program alarm that interrupted Armstrong and Aldrin was one of these. It was among a couple of dozen possible warnings that would announce themselves with a priority display and an illuminated yellow "PROG" light. When this happened, the normal display disappeared for a few seconds and was replaced by a priority display. Although far less obvious than the siren announcing a computer crisis when Margaret worked on SAGE, the yellow light and sudden change of display were dramatic enough. No one at MIT knew what had caused it. Whatever it was, it had happened at the worst possible moment.

"Something is stealing time," muttered an engineer in the SCAMA room. The 1202 code meant that there was no space in the AGC's memory for the next scheduled job. It was like a game of musical chairs, where there aren't enough chairs for the number of participants. In this

A drawing of the priority display on the DSKY as Armstrong and Aldrin saw it when they got their first program alarm—signaled by the lit "PROG" light. The alarm code is 1202, meaning their computer is overloaded.

case, the AGC suddenly had fewer blocks of memory than the frantically busy landing required. The 15 percent buffer that Bill Tindall had demanded on Black Friday was being eaten up by something that wasn't supposed to be active. But what was it?

At Mission Control, the decision about whether to keep going was up to the guidance officer, Steve Bales. He was in the middle of looking up the 1202 code when he heard from a twenty-four-year-old computer engineer named Jack Garman, who was on the radio loop in a back room. Garman had worked closely with the IL and knew the AGC's software inside and out.

"It's executive overflow," Garman said decisively. In other words, the computer had too much to do and was deleting tasks, following one of the onboard flight software's fail-safe routines. "If it does not occur again, we're fine." Garman was relying on his cheat sheet, a handwritten list of alarm codes he had assembled a few weeks earlier after similar warnings came up during simulations. Sitting next to him, the IL's Russ Larson gave a thumbs-up since he was too rattled to talk.

The back room at Mission Control during Apollo 11. Garman is second from left in the front row, wearing a dark jacket. Steve Bales, normally in the main flight control room, is standing behind the front row, also wearing a dark jacket.

Word quickly went out to the astronauts, 240,000 miles away: "We're go on that alarm!" Meaning, ignore it. Twenty seconds later, there was another 1202 alarm. The problem hadn't gone away.

• • •

Meanwhile, aboard the lunar module Buzz Aldrin was pretty sure he knew what was happening. The LM had two radars: one for landing and one for rendezvous with the CM. "You're making a descent; you need the landing radar," he later explained. "You're making a rendezvous; you need the rendezvous radar. But you don't need to mix the two." However, Aldrin *had* mixed the two. During training he followed an unofficial checklist in his head to "hurry things up." One thing he liked to do was turn the rendezvous radar on so it would be active in case of an abort during the landing phase, which was a frequent occurrence during simulations. Otherwise the rendezvous radar wasn't needed, and if the abort didn't happen, he would switch it off before landing—again, as part of his routine in the simulator. He did this to save time so he could get in as many practice sessions as possible, and it drove mission controllers crazy.

"He took this shortcut over and over again in his simulations just prior to the actual Apollo 11 mission," Margaret later wrote. "But during the real Apollo 11 mission Aldrin forgot for a moment that he was in a real flight," and he had the rendezvous radar switch on when it should have been off. This caused the memory overload—the executive overflow—which triggered a 1202 program alarm. In fact, it triggered a series of 1202 and 1201 alarms, which were similar. Aldrin surely knew the cause, but he was so busy with the landing that he didn't reset the switch until the alarm had interrupted the crew five times.

• • •

Luckily, the onboard flight software was handling the problem. Deep inside the AGC, the lightning-fast execution of tasks was backing up like a clogged pipe. As the computer's operating system, called Executive, raced through its sequence of jobs, it hadn't yet finished when it was time to repeat the cycle. This caused a backup in the workload and an executive overflow alarm, simultaneously triggering priority displays and software restarts.

Steve Bales explained executive overflow this way: "What it really means is, 'Hey, Bud, I had too much to do that last second. I didn't get it all done, and I hope that I've done the most important things. And it's up to you to figure out if I've done the most important things, because I'm going on. I can't stop.'"

In order of priority, error detection and recovery in real time came first since it acted like a combined smoke alarm and fire department, looking out for an emergency and instantly responding to it. Next in order of importance were flight control and guidance. These kept the LM stable and the trajectory on course, using the fuel as efficiently as possible. One of the biggest problems with landing on the Moon was getting down before running out of gas. Most people thought the astronauts were doing the piloting—steering the vehicle and adjusting the throttle, which determined the amount of fuel going to the engine. But the software was really doing this. No human could possibly have guided the LM manually from orbit to the surface before the propellant tanks ran dry.

So priority scheduling kept the LM flying safely through a series of executive overflow alarms. With each alarm, the AGC instantaneously restarted the software, and the software resumed the highest priority functions, throwing out any elements that weren't absolutely necessary. This included the DSKY, which went blank for ten seconds. The screen was the crew's primary source of information about the LM's altitude, velocity, and descent rate, which were hard to judge out the window. Armstrong later remarked that he never expected the DSKY to come back. In any event, he and Aldrin knew that the software was doing its job—concentrating on what was critical. Consequently, they were eerily calm for two people heading down to the Moon with warning lights flashing.

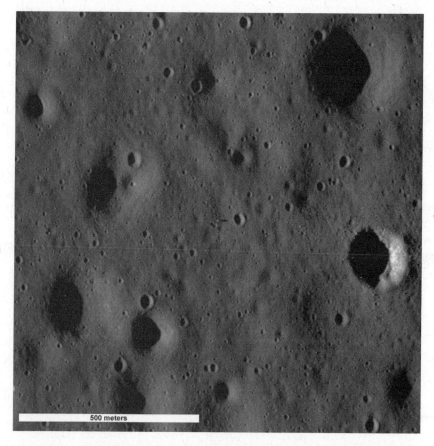

500 meters

Overhead view of the Apollo 11 landing site. The scene is two-thirds of a mile on each side. The lunar module was coming from the right and heading for the rim of the dark crater at center right. Armstrong extended the flight, running low on fuel and aiming for a level spot near the center of the frame.

Mission control also stayed cool. Unlike the FORGET IT episode eighteen months earlier, when controllers switched off the AGC and improvised procedures, this time they trusted the software. Reassuringly, Garman kept announcing, "We're go!" after each of five executive overflow alarms over a span of four and a half minutes.

By the last of the alarms, the LM had slowed to roughly fifty miles per hour and was nearing the ground. Then Armstrong spotted trouble ahead.

Margaret lecturing after Apollo, 1980s.

CHAPTER 27

COMPUTER "ERROR"

EARLIER IN THE LANDING PHASE, ARMSTRONG looked out the window and saw landmarks passing by slightly earlier than he expected—as if you are on a car trip and find you are ahead of schedule. This may sound like a good thing, but it meant the LM would overshoot its planned landing site, which had been carefully chosen to be as flat and crater free as possible. Apollo 11 was heading for rough country.

And that is exactly what Armstrong saw out the window after the program alarms cleared. The software knew nothing about the overshoot, and instead of steering for the planned landing zone, the autopilot was now guiding the craft toward the boulder-strewn rim of a large crater the size of two football fields.

"Pretty rocky area," Neil muttered.

Landing amid the car-sized rocks would have been risky. So Armstrong flipped a switch to turn on a semiautomated mode, which let him control the rate of descent. This allowed him to fly beyond the boulders to a safer spot, while the software handled the throttle and other flying functions. However, this step pushed the LM to the limit of its propellant supply.

Unrattled by the recent alarms, Mission Control was growing increasingly concerned by the fuel situation. As controllers relayed declining readings to the crew, Neil flew past the big crater toward a level area in the distance, "about the size of a big house lot," he later said. Meanwhile, Buzz read him the changing numbers on the restored DSKY.

"400 feet . . . down at 9 . . . 58 forward." This meant the LM was at an altitude of four hundred feet, descending at nine feet per second, while traveling forward at fifty-eight feet per second, or about forty miles per hour. The ship was behaving like a helicopter on its final approach. By this point Neil had taken over almost complete control, and there was no way to give it back to the computer. He and Buzz were on their own. Even Mission Control stopped talking to keep distractions to a minimum.

A minute later, the LM was down to two hundred feet.

"I got a good spot," Armstrong said half aloud.

It took another minute to get there. On the way, they received the thirty-second fuel warning from Mission Control—meaning they had to land as soon as possible.

Twelve seconds later, they did.

• • •

The SCAMA room erupted in cheers. There was also a perceptible change in the unusually still air as people started breathing again. The AGC and its software had performed a seeming miracle. Humans were on the Moon at last!

It was "maybe the most exciting moment of my life," Margaret said many years later. "Everything came rushing through my mind"—

Buzz Aldrin on the Moon with scientific instruments he has just deployed.

the countless meetings, the sleepless nights, the million and one steps that she and her colleagues had taken to get to this point.

However, someone from Mission Control was immediately on the phone to MIT. "What were those alarms?" he demanded to know. Some of the controllers certainly knew about Aldrin's practice with the rendezvous radar switch, but this high-level official didn't. "We're launching in 24 hours and we're not going with alarms. We must have an operational computer." As the entire world focused on the televised spectacle of Armstrong and Aldrin climbing out of the LM and stepping onto the Moon, the hardware people at the IL were busy trying to track down the source of the overload. "We tried every anomalous condition," said Fred Martin. "We examined the executive code, the alarm mechanism, and the fundamental algorithms. We worked all night and time was running short. Our NASA buddies called us every 15–30 minutes anticipating, demanding a solution. We had to find it. We re-covered old ground, new ground, brainstorms, crazy ideas, anything."

The next morning, a possible answer walked through the door. George Silver was an IL engineer who had seen the rendezvous radar steal time in previous tests, draining exactly the amount of memory that had plagued Apollo 11. He had called the problem to the attention of LM engineers, but the word never got around. This observation seemed unrelated to Aldrin's mis-set switch, but it coincidentally involved the rendezvous radar. So based on Silver's clue and their knowledge of Aldrin's simulator habits, Mission Control instructed the two astronauts to disable the rendezvous radar before takeoff. They wouldn't need it until they were in orbit when any extra load on the computer could be easily handled.

After the mission, experts studied the program alarms and their cause and came up with conflicting theories on precisely who or what was at fault. Was the culprit the switch setting, the power supply, a disobedient astronaut, the checklist, or some other factor? Or was it just a "funny little thing," showing up rarely under circumstances that were hard to predict? It almost didn't matter because the software had detected the error and recovered from it.

Histories of Apollo 11 tend to focus on the stars in the drama: the astronauts, the controllers, the spacecraft and rocket designers, and finally the machines themselves. You don't often hear about error detection and recovery in real time, implemented through human-in-the-loop priority displays, together with priority scheduling and software restarts. But these emergency programs had worked perfectly when it counted most. If the computer together with the onboard flight software "hadn't recognized this problem and taken recovery action," Margaret wrote later, "I doubt if Apollo 11 would have been the successful moon landing it was."

When she first suggested these safeguards, some of her colleagues had balked. They believed they could make better use of the computer's limited memory for their own needs, such as additional accuracy in the guidance and rendezvous equations. They thought that software should stick to traditional calculations, not visionary programs designed to get the astronauts out of a jam. In fact, such uses were thought by some experts to be a waste because "astronauts don't make mistakes." Their confidence was shattered by the Lauren incident on Apollo 8, not to mention by Buzz Aldrin and his absent-minded radar-switch setting on Apollo 11.

As usual, Margaret was not just being visionary in presenting her ideas. Anyone can come up with a bright idea. She was being decisive. As she put it, "Boldness has genius, power, and magic in it."

• • •

Three weeks after Apollo 11 returned to Earth, President Richard Nixon hosted a state dinner honoring Armstrong, Aldrin, and Collins. Over fourteen hundred people attended. Also recognized that night were the controllers in Houston. In particular, Nixon singled out Steve Bales. "This is the young man, when the computers seemed to be confused and when he could have said 'Stop,' or when he could have said 'Wait,' said, 'Go.'" Nixon didn't realize that Jack Garman was the one yelling "Go!" But Garman was too modest to claim any credit. When a NASA publication reported Nixon's tribute, the account was even more dismissive of the AGC and its software, praising Mission Control's "decision to proceed with lunar landing when computers failed."

President Richard Nixon at the ceremony honoring the Apollo 11 crew with the Presidential Medal of Freedom. Left to right: Aldrin, Collins, Nixon, Armstrong, and Vice-President Spiro Agnew.

"Computers . . . confused." "Computers failed." It was the same old story. In coming years, Margaret tried to set the story straight, patiently explaining her team's extraordinary achievement. "The design we had for taking care of errors *worked*—beautifully," she pointed out on one occasion.

Her boss Dick Battin also had to fight this battle.

"We did get the alarm, right?" NASA's head of manned space flight casually asked him one day. "So that was an error, right?"

"No," explained Battin firmly, "the alarm was merely telling you that the computer was . . . shutting down activities . . . and restarting those activities which were absolutely essential. There was a mistake, and the mistake was that somebody had left a switch in the wrong position."

At Nixon's state dinner, nobody thought to honor MIT.

Apollo 17 takes off on
the last Apollo mission
to the Moon, 1972.

CHAPTER 28

"WAKE UP, MARGARET!"

"WAKE UP, MARGARET! IT'S TAKING OFF!"

Margaret felt like Dorothy in *The Wizard of Oz*, being shaken to consciousness after exploits that could only happen in a dream.

But it was real. Three and a half miles away, the largest rocket in the world was blasting off on the final Apollo expedition to the Moon. It was just after midnight in the early hours of December 7, 1972. Apollo 8 had launched four years earlier. Since then, seven other missions had made the lunar journey. Five had landed. Margaret had played a leading role in each, but she had never seen a launch until now.

"We have a liftoff, and it's lighting up the area," said the voice over the loudspeaker. "It's just like daylight here at Kennedy Space Center as the Saturn V is moving off the pad. It has now cleared the tower."

The timing of this mission, Apollo 17, meant that it was launching at night. In fact, it had been delayed for two and a half hours and Margaret was taking advantage of the lull to catch up on much-needed sleep. She had been working grueling hours on Apollo for weeks, months—years, really.

As the count neared zero, her friends noticed she was asleep and woke her up. They were outside on bleachers and far enough from the launchpad so that the sound didn't reach them until nearly twenty seconds after the mighty engines ignited. The light was like the rising Sun, and the noise was like a million freight trains. The experience was blinding, bone shaking, and unforgettable.

Margaret (lower left) and colleagues in the SCAMA room during Apollo 17, the final mission in the Apollo lunar landing program.

• • •

Doc Draper was also at the launch. The night before, he had hosted a dinner for other IL staff members who were in town. It was part celebration, part funeral. He wondered aloud what challenge could possibly top the exhilaration of the Apollo program. He needed another impossible problem to solve. There were certainly plenty of those—poverty, world peace, saving the environment—but he wanted something as magical and mythic as going to the Moon. Long afterward, a former IL engineer made a similar lament: "I've spent the last twenty years looking for another Apollo, and I never could find one. Why isn't there anything like that again?"

Doc Draper toasts his team at the Apollo 17 splashdown party.

• • •

Margaret stayed on at the Instrumentation Lab, serving as an assistant director through the end of the lunar missions. She continued through the Skylab program, which was an Earth-orbiting space station, and Apollo-Soyuz, which was a joint flight in Earth orbit by

American astronauts and Soviet cosmonauts. All used a command module and the AGC. Flying in 1975, Apollo-Soyuz marked the end of the Cold War competition in space between the United States and Soviet Union. Historians believe a key reason that American astronauts got to the Moon first (Soviet space travelers never got there at all) was America's lead in computer technology. There were computers at the launch center, computers at Mission Control, computers at the contractors, computers at the tracking stations, and of course the miniature AGC in the spacecraft. Among all these electronic brains, the only computer that never failed was the AGC. In thousands of hours of manned spaceflight, no software errors were known to have occurred. The achievement is unique in computer history. "Nobody can believe it to this day," Margaret noted.

Bill Tindall noted it too. On his memo approving the final batch of AGC lunar mission software, NASA's crusty troubleshooter lavished high praise on the IL software team, scribbling, "Behold these people, for they have created perfection!!!"

Today, much is made of the fact that an electronic toy given away with a fast-food meal has more processing power than the AGC. Such comparisons imply that the AGC was ancient technology. But that's like equating a kindergarten art project to a painting by Leonardo da Vinci. Both use similar materials. But one is a masterpiece, with not a brushstroke out of place. In the AGC those brushstrokes were the lines of code, painstakingly written and rewritten by Margaret and her colleagues. Many of the innovations that people take for granted in computers today were pioneered by the AGC and its software: most importantly, integrated circuits (also called computer chips), along with error detection and recovery in real time, flexibility in executing tasks, and the human-in-the-loop features of the priority displays.

Asked in later years about her proudest accomplishment, Margaret replied with midwestern modesty, "I don't think I'm comfortable with the word *proud*, but the most memorable, the most exciting, the thing I think back to probably more often is that whole experience with Apollo 11."

• • •

Margaret didn't find another Project Apollo, but she came close, throwing herself into the problem of banishing software bugs from computer programs. In 1976, she started her own company dedicated to applying the lessons of Apollo to engineering and commercial coding projects. Through her experiences with this venture and a later, even more ambitious enterprise, she created Universal Systems Language, designed "to solve problems considered next to impossible to solve with traditional approaches."

Combining a variety of techniques in mathematics and computer science, USL allows coders to construct system software as they would a building, with a secure foundation and a sturdy structure. Any piece of code that meets the right standards fits into it—with no problems, errors, or bugs. Margaret called the principle "development before the fact," meaning that the overall plan is developed in detail before tackling the individual pieces. Oddly enough, this is not the usual practice in software engineering. However, Margaret's philosophy was to do things the way they did in the Upper Peninsula, with as little wasted effort as possible.

• • •

After the Moon landings, the astronauts were famous, the rocket designers were famous, even members of the Mission Control team were famous. But practically no one knew about the computer and the software engineers who had played such a crucial role in the missions. That may be because the Moon landing itself never ceased to be impressive, but the AGC looked less and less remarkable as computer technology advanced at a rapid pace in the decades that followed Apollo. A generation after the flights, historians looked back and realized that the IL had accomplished a miracle with 1960s technology—and not least with the software. A large part of the credit goes to Margaret Hamilton.

On November 22, 2016, Margaret stood in the East Room of the White House to receive the Presidential Medal of Freedom, the nation's highest civilian honor. President Barack Obama told the story of the program alarms that signaled the AGC had everything under control. The software was so ingeniously written that at first not even Margaret and the other programmers realized there was really nothing to worry about: Apollo 11 could safely land. "Keep in mind," said Obama, "that, at this time, software engineering wasn't even a field yet. There were no textbooks to follow, so, as Margaret says, 'There was no choice but to be pioneers.'"

The president pointed out that Margaret was also a trailblazer in being a woman in her field. "She symbolizes the generation of unsung women who helped send humankind into space." As usual, Margaret rarely thought about this. Her father and grandfather had taught her that such things didn't matter. Naturally, she had to fight the ingrained attitudes in others that limited opportunities for women, but somehow she had broken through. She wasn't sure how.

That afternoon at the White House, Margaret mingled with the other recipients of the Medal of Freedom. Bill Gates was there.

Forty-seven years after Apollo 11, President Barack Obama presents Margaret the Presidential Medal of Freedom for helping fly the first astronauts to the Moon.

He was the software genius who had helped create the personal computer industry. As a teenager, his mentor had been John Norton, only a few years after the bug detective's job eyeballing code for the AGC. Actor Tom Hanks was also there. Among his movie roles, he had played astronaut Jim Lovell in a film about Apollo 13—Lovell's second-worst emergency after the Lauren bug. Diana Ross was there too. Her musical group, the Supremes, had been one of Margaret's favorites when she was at MIT. Also present was basketball player Michael Jordan, towering more than a foot above Margaret.

Twenty-one illustrious Americans were honored that afternoon, including Grace Hopper, a groundbreaker in many aspects of computing. She was no longer alive, but she was a legend in computer science, having inspired the first widely used business programming language that made computers a vital tool in the world's economy. Margaret had met Hopper once about an important software issue. It was all strictly business, and the fact that they were two of the few prominent women in the field didn't come up.

• • •

All her life Margaret believed it shouldn't matter that she was a woman. But it mattered to other people. One day a colleague noted that on the organization chart for the IL at the time of Apollo, she was the only top manager who was female. It was hard to tell because the managers were all listed by their last name plus initials. She was M. H. Hamilton. "That's interesting," she thought. "I never realized that."

Margaret looked no farther, but if she had surveyed all the top jobs connected with the historic effort to send humans to the Moon, no other woman held as senior a post as she did. Among a sea of male faces designing rockets, riding rockets, and calling the shots in every part of the project, she was the only member of her sex who had played a central, indispensable role. The trip to the Moon could not have happened without her—at least not as flawlessly as it did. In her own way, Margaret was the woman in the Moon.

ACKNOWLEDGMENTS

WRITING A BOOK IS BOTH A CHALLENGE AND A pleasure. This book has been pure pleasure due to the many hours of conversations with Margaret Hamilton. I thank Margaret for telling me her fascinating life story, answering my questions, and correcting my drafts. Much in here is beyond her direct experience, and I alone am responsible for errors.

Claire Dorsett, then an editor at Roaring Brook, started me on this project. Emily Feinberg picked up the baton after Claire left for a career with science museums. Emily has been a dream editor: patient, insightful, and decisive. Backing her up with warmth and skill has been her assistant, Emilia Sowersby. I am also grateful to designer Veronica Mang, production editor Jennifer Healey, copyeditor Sherri Schmidt, and cover illustrator Elizabeth Baddeley.

This is my eighth book as the author. Over the years I have worn several hats in publishing—as printer, book designer, editor, photo researcher, and, for a while, head of a small press. I have loved every aspect of it and especially the many talented and congenial people in the trade. A book couldn't exist without the author's manuscript, but it also couldn't exist without innumerable others who do their jobs with professional mastery. They are my collaborators, and I thank them all.

My wife, Susie, has been my soul mate in publishing and other endeavors for a long time. My first book was dedicated to her and our older son, who was then a toddler. This book is dedicated to *his* son, and the son and daughter of our younger son. May this new generation embrace life with the enthusiasm, humility, and sense of adventure shown by the heroine of this book.

Margaret poses in a mock-up of the command module.

Margaret sizes up the Apollo Guidance Computer software, 1969.

MARGARET HAMILTON TIME LINE

1936   Born Margaret Elaine Heafield in Paoli, Indiana.

1946   Family moves to Michigan's Upper Peninsula.

1951–1956   Summer job at the Arcadian Copper Mine.

1954   Graduates from Hancock High School, Hancock, Michigan. Enrolls at the University of Michigan, Ann Arbor. Later transfers to Earlham College.

1957   Soviet Union launches world's first artificial satellite, Sputnik 1, opening the space age.

1958   Margaret graduates from Earlham, majoring in mathematics. Marries Jim Hamilton.

1958–1959   Teaches high school math and French in Indiana.

1959   Moves to Boston area so she and Jim can attend graduate school. Daughter, Lauren, born. (Margaret never does go to graduate school.)

1959–1961   Works as computer programmer for MIT meteorology professor Edward Lorenz.

1961 President Kennedy commits U.S. to land a man on the Moon by the end of the decade. Called Project Apollo.

1961–1963 Margaret serves as a programmer on the SAGE air defense project.

1963–1965 Programmer for the MIT meteorology department.

1965 Begins work at the MIT Instrumentation Lab, helping write onboard flight software for the Apollo Guidance Computer.

1968 Put in charge of all onboard flight software for the AGC.

1968 Apollo 8, guided by the AGC, is the first mission to carry astronauts around the Moon.

1969 Apollo 11 is the first manned mission to land on the Moon, thanks to crucial coding contributions by Margaret.

1976 Margaret leaves the IL for the private sector, starting her own companies.

2003 Receives NASA's Exceptional Space Act Award for leading the Apollo onboard flight software team.

2016 Awarded Presidential Medal of Freedom by President Obama.

NOTES

QUOTATIONS FROM MARGARET HAMILTON AND incidents from her life that are not referenced below are from the author's interviews with her on the following dates: February 26 and May 11, 2018; March 19, September 10, and December 13, 2019; February 13 and September 24, 2020; January 8, February 17, March 12, May 14, June 23, July 21, September 23, and October 22, 2021; and January 5, February 22, and March 11, 2022. The author also interviewed Hugh Blair-Smith on October 14, 2019.

Feel free to contact the author with questions at *richardsmaurer@ gmail.com* (note the middle initial, "s").

Abbreviations

AGCHP = Apollo Guidance Computer History Project

JSC = Johnson Space Center Oral History Project

ix   "She was the Goddess of Software": Blair-Smith, *Left Brains*, location 2642.

xii   "could not be convinced": The Locke-Ober meeting is described in McDougall, *The Heavens and the Earth*, p. 301.

xiii $40 billion: Due to superb management, Project Apollo would cost a third less.

xvi "Of course, we'll shut the computer off": Ramon Alonso, in "Automatic vs. Manual," AGCHP Conference 1, July 27, 2001, authors .library.caltech.edu/5456/1/hrst.mit.edu/hrs/apollo/public/conference1 /automatic-manual.htm.

xvi "crazy": Cline Frasier, introduction, AGCHP Conference 1, July 27, 2001, authors.library.caltech.edu/5456/1/hrst.mit.edu/hrs/apollo/public /conference1/frasier-intro.htm.

xvi the space agency had decreed: Mindell, *Digital Apollo*, p. 158.

5 digging a hole to get there: Hamilton, interview by Brock, Computer History Museum, p. 17.

7 the Ojibwa warrior Hiawatha: The legendary Ojibwa warrior was really named Nanabozho. For the purposes of his poem, Longfellow preferred the euphony of Hiawatha, who historically united the five warring Haudenosaunee (Iroquois) nations around New York.

8 *"Once a warrior, very angry"*: Longfellow, "Hiawatha's Childhood," in *The Song of Hiawatha*, p. 42.

9 In ancient Greece, one legend: ní Mheallaigh, *Moon in Greek and Roman Imagination*, pp. 182–83. The Alutiiq legend is known as "The Girl Who Married the Moon" and is recounted in Golder, "Tales from Kodiak Island," pp. 28–31.

11 produced the most detailed lunar map: Whitaker, *Mapping and Naming the Moon*, pp. 78–80.

15 *Is this for certain the way things go?*: Heafield, "Destination," in *Beachcomber*, p. 13.

17 "My mother used to get upset": Teitz, *Nice Girl Like You*, pp. 245–46.

23 "Our mine is real!": For details on the mine, see Juntunen, "Tourist Mines Pay Off Big." Also see "Unique Journey Leads to Adit of Copper Mine," *Ironwood Daily Globe*, August 2, 1952, p. 3.

25 "like a slot machine on a binge": Juntunen, "Tourist Mines Pay Off Big."

31 "18,500 Enrollment Expected": The headline appeared on Jim Dygert's story in the *Michigan Daily*, September 15, 1954.

32 "to keep their hands off my women!": Tobin, "Dean Bacon's Demise," *Michigan Today*, October 22, 2014.

35 "a unity of tone": Trueblood, *Idea of a College*, p. 27.

35 "A mountain is far superior": Trueblood, *Idea of a College*, p. 11.

37 a winning bid of $64: Humes, "Chest Drive Surges Over $800 Goal," *Earlham Post*, April 26, 1955, p. 4.

38 teaching children with disabilities: "Lovelies for Queen," *Earlham Post*, October 11, 1956, p. 4.

38 "She is known on campus": Earlham College, *Sargasso* 1957, p. 86.

39 "If you can't solve it": Hamilton, interview by Brock, Computer History Museum, p. 42.

41 "Everybody looked up to her": "Look Back," *Earlhamite*, Summer 2019, p. 47.

42 "I am most disturbed": Kenschaft, "Charlotte Angas Scott," p. 197.

43 "wasted her education by majoring in men's courses": Texas State Teachers Association, *Texas Outlook* 17, December 1933, p. 31.

45 "No truly devout person": Trueblood, *Philosophy of Religion*, p. 57.

46 Charlotte Angas Scott: Scott's life is covered in Kenschaft, "Charlotte Angas Scott," pp. 193–203.

50 "Communists talk abstractly": Root, *Collectivism on the Campus*, p. 15.

51 "one of the most beloved and effective teachers on the Earlham staff": Hamm, *Earlham College*, pp. 224–25.

53 "The United States is losing the cold war": Root, *Brainwashing*, p. 3.

53 In a talk to students: Root's talk is reported in "Alternative to Conservatism," *Earlham Post*, April 26, 1957, p. 3.

55 "Root attempts to preserve": "Alternative to Conservatism," *Earlham Post*.

57 "Do people ever date": "Thimk!" [*sic*], *Earlham Post*, May 2, 1957, p. 2.

58 "The fact that the ordinary residential college": Trueblood, *Idea of a College*, pp. 115–16.

65 "A few students and users will develop": Tukey, "Teaching of Concrete Mathematics," p. 3.

68 the staff called this process "programming": Grier, "The ENIAC," p. 52.

68 "The assumption was that only women would do this": Jean Jennings Bartik, panel discussion, UNIVAC Conference, Session 2, May 17, 1990, pp. 60–61.

69 "If the ENIAC's administrators had known": Jean Jennings Bartik, *Pioneer Programmer* (Truman State, 2013), p. 557, as cited in Isaacson, *Innovators*, p. 100.

72 "He loved that computer": Sokol, "Hidden Heroines of Chaos."

73 One expert estimated: Richardson, *Weather Prediction*, p. 219.

74 a program like this: The example (corrected) is from Smillie, "Programming Then and Now," p. 5.

77 It made a *huge* difference: Lorenz, *Essence of Chaos*, pp. 134–36.

77 "butterfly effect": Lorenz, *Essence of Chaos*, pp. 14–15.

77 Lorenz's pioneer report: Lorenz, "Statistical Prediction of Solutions." Margaret is credited on p. 634.

83 250-ton AN/FSQ-7: Ulmann, *AN/FSQ-7*, p. 2. The letters were generally thought to stand for Army-Navy Fixed Special eQuipment. But according to military naming conventions, the Q denoted a special, multipurpose function.

83 seventy-five thousand instructions per second: By contrast, a 2020s smartphone fits in a shirt pocket, performs billions of instructions per second, and consumes a watt or two.

85 "Salaries Open!": Philco Techrep Division, display ad, *Boston Globe*, April 30, 1961, p. 18-A.

89 the hackers had surreptitiously rewired: The story of Margaret and the hackers is told in Levy, *Hackers*, chap. 5.

93 The new law didn't take full effect: The Civil Rights Act of 1964 took full effect on July 2, 1965.

93 "overall design responsibility": MIT Instrumentation Laboratory, display ad, *Boston Globe*, October 18, 1964, p. A-17. The ads also appeared in the *Globe* on November 5, p. 45, and November 6, p. 39.

94 "I thought that was very exciting": Teitz, *Nice Girl Like You*, p. 235.

96 "We accept the challenge": Trueblood, *Idea of a College*, p. 59.

103 According to Doc, the conversation went like this: The conversation between Webb and Draper is slightly adapted from Battin, interview by Wright, JSC. Other versions of the exchange are in Wildenberg,

Hot Spot of Invention, p. 205; MacKenzie, *Inventing Accuracy*, p. 190; and Wilford, "Charles S. Draper."

109 at a distance of seven miles: The target zone for the first Apollo landing had a diameter of ten miles. A basketball hoop has a diameter of eighteen inches. Given that the Moon is 240,000 miles away, the corresponding distance to the hoop would be seven miles. Later Apollo missions had much smaller target zones, requiring even more precise guidance.

110 guidance would be much more flexible: Tomayko, *Computers in Space-flight*, p. 30.

113 he had no more than five programmers: Battin's reminiscences are in Battin, interview by Wright, JSC.

114 "Well, how many people": The following conversation is slightly adapted from Battin, interview by Wright, JSC.

114 more than four hundred: Johnson and Giller, *The Software Effort*, pp. 20–21.

115 Ada, Countess of Lovelace: For Ada's story, see Isaacson, *Innovators*, chap. 1. The verse is from Byron, *Childe Harold's Pilgrimage*, canto 3, stanza 1.

120 sewing machine: Some of Cambridge's innovations can be found at MacDonald, "Innovation in Cambridge."

122 One of Margaret's first assignments: Margaret's introduction to inertial navigation is noted by Alex Kosmala in "Role of Personal Background," AGCHP Conference 2, September 14, 2001, authors.library.caltech.edu /5456/1/hrst.mit.edu/hrs/apollo/public/conference2/background.htm.

122 the coordinate system used to guide Apollo: Apollo used Earth- or Moon-centered coordinates, depending on where the spacecraft was in its journey. See NASA, *Project Apollo Coordinate System Standards*.

123 FORGET IT: Margaret's recollections of the lunar landmark tables and FORGET IT are from her introduction, AGCHP Conference 1, July 27, 2001, authors.library.caltech.edu/5456/1/hrst.mit.edu/hrs /apollo/public/conference1/hamilton-intro.htm.

125 first unmanned test of the lunar module: The test was designated Apollo 5 and is recounted in the fifteen-minute NASA documentary, *The Apollo 5*

Mission. The FORGET IT episode is detailed in Kranz, *Failure Is Not an Option*, chap. 11.

126 Doc Draper was following the flight: Fred Martin, in "Simulation and Training," AGCHP Conference 1, July 27, 2001, authors.library.caltech .edu/5456/1/hrst.mit.edu/hrs/apollo/public/conference1/simulation.htm.

129 "an incorrect computer instruction": Kranz, *Failure Is Not an Option*, p. 218.

129 "a software error": Kelly, *Moon Lander*, p. 194.

129 "The inability of an onboard computer to cope": NASA, *The Apollo 5 Mission*, 14:19.

131 "like a finely tuned orchestra": Hamilton, "What the Errors Tell Us," p. 33.

132 "Who the hell was that guy up front?": Lickly, "Lecture on Polaris and Apollo," starting at 34:34.

133 "You can't build a digital autopilot": Scott, "Apollo Guidance Computer."

134 "Inevitably, they will resist anything that's automatic": Joseph Gavin, in "Automatic vs. Manual," AGCHP Conference 1, July 27, 2001, authors .library.caltech.edu/5456/1/hrst.mit.edu/hrs/apollo/public/conference1 /automatic-manual.htm.

138 "I will never forget": Hamilton, "Apollo On-Board Flight Software."

139 Their worry was that the switchover: Whittell, "First Woman."

144 On the next page is one of Johnson's equations: White and Johnson, "Approximate Solutions for Flight-Path Angle," p. 6, equation 10. For Johnson's life in full, see Shetterly, *Hidden Figures*.

147 *Fifteen birds in five firtrees*: Tolkien, *Hobbit*, p. 123.

148 "would come running to find out": Hamilton, "What the Errors Tell Us," p. 32.

148 John Norton: Norton's story is covered in Goodman, "Practicing Safe Software."

150 "I've got to find out what this is": Hayes, "Moonshot Computing."

153 The IL staff had already figured out: Blair-Smith, *Left Brains*, location 2494. The final version of the Apollo Guidance Computer had 36,864 16-bit words of fixed memory and 2,048 words of erasable memory. In

today's terms, a low-resolution photo sent with an email or a text message would fill *all* the AGC's memory. See "Defining Computer 'Power,'" in O'Brien, *Apollo Guidance Computer*, pp. 4–7.

154   "There are a number of us who feel": Tindall, memo 66-FM1–68, May 31, 1966. Bill Tindall's folksy, often devastating memos were widely known as "Tindallgrams." A selection from the hundreds of Tindallgrams is available at "Tindallgrams: The Snarky Memos of Apollo's Unsung Genius," tindallgrams.net.

154   "How can you possibly do this?": Ed Copps, in "Bill Tindall and Conflicts Within Apollo," AGCHP Conference 4, September 6, 2002, authors.library.caltech.edu/5456/1/hrst.mit.edu/hrs/apollo/public /conference4/tindall.htm.

155   a 15 percent buffer: Blair-Smith, *Left Brains*, location 3481.

156   "She saw me playing that way": For quotes and a description of the incident, see Hamilton, "In Their Own Words" and "They Worried."

157   not to tell their friends: Battin, "Some Funny Things Happened," p. 3.

157   "It was an ongoing joke for a long time": Snyder and Henry, *Fluency with Information Technology*, pp. 173–74.

159   "to perform very well for us": Tindall, memo 67-FM1–9, January 23, 1967.

159   sometime in 1968: For the optimistic outlook on the eve of Apollo 1, see McElheny, "Moon Program Ahead of Schedule."

161   "Will this be the end of Apollo?": Blair-Smith, *Left Brains*, location 2916.

161   some five thousand changes: Collins, *Carrying the Fire*, p. 304.

161   "a disturbing number of flaws": Blair-Smith, *Left Brains*, location 2947.

163   Margaret was managing the teams: Hoag, "History of Apollo Guidance," p. 10.

166   "Is it possible to be accurate all of the time?": Cornell and Heafield, *Principles and Practices for the Legal Secretary*, p. 103.

167   "If you cannot work with love": Kahlil Gibran, *The Prophet* (New York: Knopf, 1923), p. 33, in Cornell and Heafield, p. 151.

168   "one of the few mortals": Krueger, "Rare Mortal."

169 "Florid, with greying crew cut": Krueger, "Rare Mortal."

169 *Good night*: Heafield, *Beachcomber*, p. 15.

169 misheard "poetry" as "poultry": "K. Heafield, 57, Former Garden Resident Dies," *Escanaba Daily Press*, December 19, 1967, p. 2.

174 "I turned to the guy next to me": Davidson and Riley, "Navigation Computer," 30:24.

175 within eighty-seven miles: Or 75.6 nautical miles in the units used by Apollo. See Orloff and Harland, *Apollo*, p. 203.

177 a fragile daisy chain of events: Collins, *Carrying the Fire*, p. 381.

178 like a virtuoso pianist: LBJ Library, "Apollo 8 Reunion." The story of Lovell's DSKY error starts at 41:00.

178 "Oops!": The crew's conversation with Mission Control from the time of Lovell's mistake to its resolution can be found from 106:27:22 in "Day 5: The Green Team" to 115:17:22 in "Day 5: The Maroon Team," at Woods and O'Brien, Apollo 8 Flight Journal. Lovell's "Oops!" was not transmitted. history.nasa.gov/afj/ap08fj/index.html.

185 Lovell reportedly said that his most frightening moment: Cline Frasier, introduction, AGCHP Conference 1, July 27, 2001, authors.library.caltech .edu/5456/1/hrst.mit.edu/hrs/apollo/public/conference1/frasier-intro.htm.

188 "I pretty much had to calculate": Aldrin and Abraham, *Magnificent Desolation*, p. 49. Aldrin refers to the "Mark One Cranium Computer" in Aldrin and McConnell, *Men from Earth*, p. 154.

191 her salary was doubled: Wang, "NASA Pioneer Speaks."

191 "When I took over": Hamilton, "They Worried."

192 "the questions he asked": Dan Lickly, in "Interaction with Astronauts," AGCHP Conference 2, September 14, 2001, authors.library.caltech.edu /5456/1/hrst.mit.edu/hrs/apollo/public/conference2/astronauts.htm.

193 with an unusual taste for poetry: Collins's love for poetry is expressed in his preface to the 2019 edition of his book *Carrying the Fire*, p. xxiii.

193 three miles of wire and just over three thousand cores: Shirriff, "Software Woven into Wire."

193 erasable memory: The erasable memory used the brand-new technology of integrated circuits (ICs), with each of the AGC's 2,800 silicon ICs

having three transistors. A single IC in the 2020s can have billions of transistors.

194 March 28: See the cover page on "Colossus 2A," Assembly and Operation Information, April 1, 1969, ibiblio.org/apollo/ScansForConversion /Comanche055/0001.jpg.

197 "Program alarm . . . It's a 1202": Transmissions to and from Apollo 11 are from Jones and Glover, Apollo 11 Lunar Surface Journal.

197 Margaret looked over at Fred Martin: Hamilton, "Recalling the 'Giant Leap.'"

200 "It's executive overflow": "Apollo 11 Lunar Landing Audio—Flight and Guidance Loops," NASA Spaceflight.com Forum. forum.nasaspaceflight .com/index.php?topic=35230.0 (revised July 21, 2014).

202 "You're making a descent": Sington, Shadow of the Moon, starting at 56:55.

202 "hurry things up" . . . "He took this shortcut over and over again": Margaret Hamilton's subsequent discussions with Jack Garman led to the explanation given here, which is recounted in Hamilton, "Apollo On-Board Flight Software." For a brief account, see Whittell, "First Woman."

203 "What it really means is": Sharp et al., Apollo 11, starting at 23:00.

208 "about the size of a big house lot": Armstrong et al., First on the Moon, p. 242.

208 there was no way to give it back to the computer: See "The First Lunar Landing" in Jones and Glover, Apollo 11 Lunar Surface Journal, where Aldrin says, "Once we took over manually at 500 feet . . . there was no way we could give it back to the computer."

208 "maybe the most exciting moment of my life": Whittell, "First Woman."

209 "What were those alarms?": Martin, "Apollo 11." On the scramble to understand the program alarms, also see Blair-Smith, Left Brains, starting at location 3673.

210 "We tried every anomalous condition": Martin, "Apollo 11."

211 "hadn't recognized this problem": Hamilton, "Computer Got Loaded."

211 "Boldness has genius": Wang, "NASA Pioneer Speaks."

211 "This is the young man": Nixon, "Remarks at a Dinner."

212 "when computers failed": Library of Congress, *Astronautics and Aeronautics, 1969*, p. 280.

212 "The design we had for taking care of errors": Teitz, *Nice Girl Like You*, pp. 231.

213 "We did get the alarm, right?": Battin, interview by Wright, JSC.

217 "I've spent the last twenty years looking for another Apollo": Dan Lickly quotes Ray North (misidentified as Ray Martin), in AGCHP Conference 4, September 6, 2002, authors.library.caltech.edu/5456/1/hrst.mit.edu/hrs/apollo/public/conference4/nowandthen.htm.

217 serving as an assistant director: In 1970, the Instrumentation Laboratory was renamed the Charles Stark Draper Laboratory in honor of its founder.

218 no software errors were known to have occurred: Hamilton, "What the Errors Tell Us," p. 34. Also Hall, *Journey to the Moon*, p. 181.

218 "Behold these people": Tindall, memo to C. C. Kraft et al.

219 "I don't think I'm comfortable with the word *proud*": Hamilton, interview by Brock, Computer History Museum, p. 41.

219 "to solve problems considered next to impossible": Hamilton and Hackler, "Universal Systems Language," p. 34.

220 "Keep in mind": Obama, "Presentation of the Presidential Medal of Freedom."

REFERENCES

ORAL HISTORIES

Apollo Guidance Computer History Project. Dibner Institute for the History of Science and Technology, Cambridge, Mass. authors.library.caltech.edu /5456/1/hrst.mit.edu/hrs/apollo/public/documents.htm.

Battin, Richard H. Interview by Rebecca Wright. Lexington, Mass., April 18, 2000. Johnson Space Center Oral History Project, NASA. historycollection .jsc.nasa.gov/JSCHistoryPortal/history/oral_histories/BattinRH/battinrh .htm.

Garman, John R. Interviews by Kevin M. Rusnak. Houston, March 27 and April 5, 2001. Johnson Space Center Oral History Project, NASA. history collection.jsc.nasa.gov/JSCHistoryPortal/history/oral_histories/GarmanJR /garmanjr.htm.

Hamilton, Margaret H. Interview by David C. Brock. Boston, Mass., April 13, 2017. Computer History Museum. computerhistory.org/collections/catalog /102738243.

UNIVAC Conference, OH 200. Charles Babbage Institute, Smithsonian Institution, and Unisys Corporation. May 17–18, 1990, Washington, D.C. Transcript edited by Bruce H. Bruemmer. purl.umn.edu/104288.

BOOKS

Aldrin, Buzz, with Ken Abraham. *Magnificent Desolation: The Long Journey Home from the Moon.* New York: Harmony Books, 2009.

Aldrin, Buzz, and Malcolm McConnell. *Men from Earth.* New York: Bantam Books, 1989.

Blair-Smith, Hugh. *Left Brains for the Right Stuff: Computers, Space, and History.* East Bridgewater, Mass.: SDP Publishing, 2015. Kindle.

Byron, Lord. *Childe Harold's Pilgrimage: Canto the Third.* London, 1816. archive.org/details/haroldspilchilde00byrorich/page/n9/.

Collins, Michael. *Carrying the Fire: An Astronaut's Journeys,* 50th anniversary ed. New York: Farrar, Straus and Giroux, 2019. Kindle.

Cornell, Marian, and Kenneth Heafield. *Principles and Practices for the Legal Secretary.* Mundelein, Ill.: Callaghan, 1965.

Earlham College. *Sargasso* [yearbook]. Richmond, Ind., 1957, 1958.

Fishman, Charles. *One Giant Leap: The Impossible Mission That Flew Us to the Moon.* New York: Simon & Schuster, 2019.

Garden Peninsula Historical Society. *Our Heritage: Garden Peninsula, Delta County, Michigan, 1840–1980.* Garden, Mich.: Garden Peninsula Historical Society, 1982.

Hall, Eldon C. *Journey to the Moon: The History of the Apollo Guidance Computer.* Reston, Va.: American Institute of Aeronautics and Astronautics, 1996.

Hamm, Thomas D. *Earlham College: A History, 1847–1997.* Bloomington: Indiana University Press, 1997.

Heafield, Kenneth. *Beachcomber and Other Poems.* Saginaw: Michigan Poetry Chapbooks, 1964.

Houston, Rick, and Milt Heflin. *Go, Flight! The Unsung Heroes of Mission Control, 1965–1992.* Lincoln: University of Nebraska Press, 2015. Kindle.

Isaacson, Walter. *The Innovators: How a Group of Hackers, Geniuses, and Geeks Created the Digital Revolution.* New York: Simon & Schuster, 2014. Kindle.

Johnson, Howard Wesley. *Holding the Center: Memoirs of a Life in Higher Education.* Cambridge, Mass.: MIT Press, 1999.

Kelly, Thomas J. *Moon Lander: How We Developed the Apollo Lunar Module.* Washington, D.C.: Smithsonian Books, 2001.

Kenschaft, Patricia Clark. "Charlotte Angas Scott (1858–1931)." In *Women of Mathematics: A Biobibliographic Sourcebook*, edited by Louise S. Grinstein and Paul J. Campbell. New York: Greenwood Press, 1987.

Kranz, Gene. *Failure Is Not an Option: Mission Control from Mercury to Apollo 13 and Beyond.* New York: Simon & Schuster, 2000.

Levy, Steven. *Hackers: Heroes of the Computer Revolution.* Sebastopol, Calif.: O'Reilly, 2010.

Library of Congress Science and Technology Division. *Astronautics and Aeronautics, 1969: Chronology on Science, Technology, and Policy.* Washington, D.C.: NASA, 1970.

Longfellow, Henry Wadsworth. *The Song of Hiawatha.* Boston, 1855. archive.org/details/hiawathasongof00longrich/page/42/.

Lorenz, Edward N. *The Essence of Chaos.* Seattle: University of Washington Press, 1993.

MacKenzie, Donald. *Inventing Accuracy: A Historical Sociology of Nuclear Missile Guidance.* Cambridge, Mass.: MIT Press, 1990.

McDougall, Walter A. *The Heavens and the Earth: A Political History of the Space Age.* New York: Basic Books, 1985.

Mindell, David A. *Digital Apollo: Human and Machine in Spaceflight.* Cambridge, Mass.: MIT Press, 2008.

Murray, Charles, and Catherine Bly Cox. *Apollo: The Race to the Moon.* New York: Simon & Schuster, 1989.

ní Mheallaigh, Karen. *The Moon in the Greek and Roman Imagination: Myth, Literature, Science and Philosophy.* Cambridge, U.K.: Cambridge University Press, 2020.

O'Brien, Frank. *The Apollo Guidance Computer: Architecture and Operation.* Chichester, U.K.: Springer-Praxis, 2010.

Orloff, Richard W., and David M. Harland. *Apollo: The Definitive Sourcebook.* Chichester, U.K.: Springer-Praxis, 2006.

Richardson, Lewis F. *Weather Prediction by Numerical Process.* Cambridge, U.K.: Cambridge University Press, 1922.

Root, E. Merrill. *Brainwashing in the High Schools: An Examination of Eleven American History Textbooks.* New York: Devin-Adair, 1958.

Root, E. Merrill. *Collectivism on the Campus: The Battle for the Mind in American Colleges.* New York: Devin-Adair, 1956.

Shetterly, Margot Lee. *Hidden Figures: The American Dream and the Untold Story of the Black Women Mathematicians Who Helped Win the Space Race.* New York: William Morrow, 2016. Kindle.

Snyder, Lawrence, and Ray Laura Henry. *Fluency with Information Technology: Skills, Concepts & Capabilities,* 7th ed. New York: Pearson, 2018.

Teitz, Joyce. *What's a Nice Girl Like You Doing in a Place Like This?* New York: Coward, McCann & Geoghegan, 1972.

Thornburg, Opal. *Earlham: The Story of the College, 1847–1962.* Richmond, Ind.: Earlham College Press, 1963.

Tolkien, J. R. R. *The Hobbit, or There and Back Again.* London: HarperCollins, 1995.

Trueblood, David Elton. *Philosophy of Religion.* New York: Harper & Row, 1957.

Trueblood, [David] Elton. *The Idea of a College.* New York: Harper & Brothers, 1959.

Ulmann, Bernd. *AN/FSQ-7: The Computer That Shaped the Cold War.* Munich: De Gruyter Oldenbourg, 2014.

Wildenberg, Thomas. *Hot Spot of Invention: Charles Stark Draper, MIT, and the Development of Inertial Guidance and Navigation.* Annapolis, Md.: Naval Institute Press, 2019.

Woods, W. David. *How Apollo Flew to the Moon.* 2nd ed. Chichester, U.K.: Springer-Praxis, 2011.

ARTICLES, DOCUMENTS, AND VIDEOS

Apple, R. W., Jr. "Male Bastion, 108, Saved by a Boss Named Lydia." *New York Times,* February 20, 2002.

Battin, Richard H. "Some Funny Things Happened on the Way to the Moon."

Journal of Guidance, Control, and Dynamics 25, no. 1 (January-February 2002): pp. 1–7.

Bennett, Floyd V. *Apollo Experience Report: Mission Planning for Lunar Module Descent and Ascent.* Washington, D.C.: NASA, 1972. www.hq.nasa.gov/alsj /nasa-tnd-6846pt.1.pdf.

Cherry, George W. Memo to W. Kelly and Christopher Kraft, August 4, 1969, "Exegesis of the 1201 and 1202 Alarms Which Occurred During the Mission G Lunar Landing." In Blair-Smith, *Left Brains*, appendix.

Davidson, Nick, and Christopher Riley, dirs. "The Navigation Computer." Part 3 of the TV documentary *Moon Machines.* London: DOX Productions, 2008.

Dunietz, Jesse. "Why Did Obama Just Honor Bug-Free Software?" *Nautilus,* December 21, 2016. nautil.us/blog/why-did-obama-just-honor-bug_free -software.

Golder, F. A. "Tales from Kodiak Island." *Journal of American Folk-Lore* 16, no. 60 (January-March, 1903): pp. 16–31.

Goldstein, Gail, and Lee Marks. "Dean of Women's Ruling on Bermudas." *Michigan Daily,* September 22, 1954.

Goodman, Billy. "Practicing Safe Software." *Air & Space Magazine,* August 1994.

Grier, David Alan. "The ENIAC, the Verb 'To Program' and the Emergence of Digital Computers." *IEEE Annals of the History of Computing* 18, no. 1 (Spring 1996): pp. 51–55.

Hamilton, Margaret H. "The Apollo On-Board Flight Software and Apollo 11." HTI Technical Report # 2019.4.25.excerpt1.

Hamilton, Margaret H. "Computer Got Loaded." Letter to the editor. *Datamation,* March 1, 1971.

Hamilton, Margaret H. "In Their Own Words: Margaret Hamilton on Her Daughter's Simulation." Hack the Moon, Draper Laboratory. Accessed May 22, 2019. wehackthemoon.com/people/margaret-hamilton-her-daughters -simulation.

Hamilton, Margaret H. "The Language as a Software Engineer." Plenary session keynote address at 40th International Conference on Software Engineering, Göteborg, Sweden, May 31, 2018. youtu.be/ZbVOF0Uk5IU.

Hamilton, Margaret H. "Margaret Hamilton: 'They Worried That the Men Might Rebel. They Didn't.'" Interview by Zoë Corbyn. *Guardian*, July 13, 2019. theguardian.com/technology/2019/jul/13/margaret-hamilton -computer-scientist-interview-software-apollo-missions-1969-moon -landing-nasa-women.

Hamilton, Margaret H. "Priority Systems, Software Restarts and Priority Displays." HTI Technical Report # 2019.5.22.excerpt2.

Hamilton, Margaret H. In "Recalling the 'Giant Leap.'" Interviews by David Chandler. MIT News, July 17, 2009. news.mit.edu/2009/apollo-vign-0717.

Hamilton, Margaret H. "What the Errors Tell Us." *IEEE Software* 35, no. 5 (September-October 2018): pp. 32–37.

Hamilton, Margaret H., and William R. Hackler. "Universal Systems Language: Lessons Learned from Apollo," *Computer* 41, no. 12 (December 2008): pp. 34–43.

Hand, James A., ed. *Project Management, Systems Development, Abstracts and Bibliography*. Vol. 1 of *MIT's Role in Project Apollo*. Cambridge, Mass.: MIT Draper Laboratory, 1971.

Hayes, Brian. "Moonshot Computing." *American Scientist*, May-June 2019. www.americanscientist.org/article/moonshot-computing.

Hoag, David G. "The History of Apollo Guidance, Navigation, and Control." *Journal of Guidance, Control, and Dynamics* 6, no. 1 (January-February 1983): pp. 4–13.

Humes, Shirl. "Chest Drive Surges over $800." *Earlham Post*, April 26, 1955.

Johnson, Madeline S., and Donald R. Giller. *The Software Effort*. Vol. 5 of *MIT's Role in Project Apollo*. Cambridge, Mass.: MIT Draper Laboratory, 1971.

Jones, Eric M., and Ken Glover, eds. Apollo 11 Lunar Surface Journal. NASA History Division, 1995. www.hq.nasa.gov/alsj/a11/a11.html.

Juntunen, Arthur. "Tourist Mines Pay Off Big." *Detroit Free Press*, July 27, 1958.

Krueger, Pamela. "The Rare Mortal: The Campus Poet Enjoys a Luxury of Time to Spin Thoughts into a Fabric of Words." *Detroit News Sunday Magazine*, June 4, 1967.

Kutner, Joe. "Software's Giant Leap: The Story of How the Apollo Missions Changed Software." 3 parts. Medium, April 10, 2019. medium.com/softwares-giant-leap.

LBJ Presidential Library and Museum. "Apollo 8 Reunion." Apollo 40th Anniversary, Austin, Tex., April 23, 2009. youtu.be/Wa5x0T-pee0.

Lickly, Daniel. "Dan Lickly's Lecture on Polaris and Apollo," October 12, 2013. youtu.be/qtLjD1_Zg1Y.

Lorenz, Edward N. "The Statistical Prediction of Solutions of Dynamic Equations." In *Proceedings of the International Symposium on Numerical Weather Prediction in Tokyo, November 7–13, 1960*, pp. 629–635. N.p.: Meteorological Society of Japan, 1962.

MacDonald, Katie. "Innovation in Cambridge." Cambridge Historical Society, 2012. cambridgehistory.org/innovation/index-next.html.

Martin, Fred H. "Apollo 11: 25 Years Later," July 1994. Apollo 11 Lunar Surface Journal. www.hq.nasa.gov/alsj/a11/a11.1201-fm.html.

McElheny, Victor K. "Moon Program Ahead of Schedule." *Boston Globe*, January 22, 1967.

NASA. *The Apollo 5 Mission*. Film produced by A-V Corporation. Houston, 1968. youtu.be/oSnoFUFlmQg.

NASA Office of Manned Space Flight. *Project Apollo Coordinate System Standards*. Washington, D.C.: NASA, June 1965. ibiblio.org/apollo/Documents/19700076120.pdf.

Nixon, Richard M. "Remarks at a Dinner in Los Angeles Honoring the Apollo 11 Astronauts," August 13, 1969. American Presidency Project. Edited by Gerhard Peters and John T. Woolley. University of California at Santa Barbara. presidency.ucsb.edu/documents/remarks-dinner-los-angeles-honoring-the-apollo-11-astronauts.

Obama, Barack. "Remarks by the President at Presentation of the Presidential Medal of Freedom." Washington, D.C., November 22, 2016. obamawhitehouse.archives.gov/the-press-office/2016/11/22/remarks-president-presentation-presidential-medal-freedom.

Ring, Paul. "When MetroWest Went to the Moon: Area Companies Helped Apollo 11." *MetroWest Daily News*, July 19, 2009.

Scott, David. "The Apollo Guidance Computer: A User's View." Remarks at the Computer Museum, Boston, June 10, 1982. Transcript, klabs.org/history/history_docs/ech/agc_scott.pdf.

Sharp, Barbara, Elliott H. Haimoff, and Scott Stillman, writers and producers. *Apollo 11: First Steps on the Moon*. Beverly Hills, Calif.: Global Science Productions, 1999.

Shirriff, Ken. "Software Woven into Wire: Core Rope and the Apollo Guidance Computer." *Ken Shirriff's Blog*, July 4, 2019. righto.com/2019/07/software-woven-into-wire-core-rope-and.html.

Sington, David, dir. *In the Shadow of the Moon*. London: DOX Productions, 2007.

Smillie, Keith. "Programming Then and Now: From the LGP-30 to the Laptop." Semantic Scholar, June 2006. semanticscholar.org/paper/48400e88222c8b9125b605d4a2f8c92cac8cfa09.

Sokol, Joshua. "The Hidden Heroines of Chaos." *Quanta Magazine*, May 20, 2019. quantamagazine.org/the-hidden-heroines-of-chaos-20190520/.

Thomas, B. K. "Apollo 8 Proves Value of Onboard Control." *Aviation Week and Space Technology*, January 20, 1969.

Tindall, Howard W., Jr. Memo to C. C. Kraft et al., August 17, 1971, "Flight Ropes for Apollo 16 and 17." In Virtual AGC Project Document Library. ibiblio.org/apollo/Documents/16_17_flight_ropes.pdf.

Tindall, Howard W., Jr. Memo 66-FM1–68, May 31, 1966, "Apollo Spacecraft Computer Program Development Newsletter." In "Tindallgrams." Compiled by David T. Craig. web.mit.edu/digitalapollo/Documents/Chapter7/tindallgrams.pdf.

Tindall, Howard W., Jr. Memo 67-FM1–9, January 23, 1967, "Latest on the AS-206 Spacecraft Computer." In "Tindallgrams-Lumney." Apollo Lunar Surface Journal. NASA History Division. hq.nasa.gov/alsj/tindallgrams02.pdf.

Tobin, James. "Dean Bacon's Demise." *Michigan Today*, October 22, 2014. michigantoday.umich.edu/2014/10/22/dean-bacons-demise.

Tomayko, James E. *Computers in Spaceflight: The NASA Experience*. Washington, D.C.: NASA, 1988.

Tukey, John W. "The Teaching of Concrete Mathematics." *American Mathematical Monthly* 65, no. 1 (January 1958): pp. 1–9.

Wang, Mengnan. "NASA Pioneer Speaks at Convocation." *Earlham Word*, March 18, 2005.

White, Jack A., and Katherine G. Johnson. "Approximate Solutions for Flight-Path Angle of a Reentry Vehicle in the Upper Atmosphere." Technical Note D-2379. Washington, D.C.: NASA, July 1964.

Whittell, Giles. "First Woman." Tortoise, July 13, 2019. tortoisemedia.com /2019/07/13/nasa-margaret/.

Wilford, John Noble. "Charles S. Draper, Engineer; Guided Astronauts to Moon." *New York Times*, July 27, 1987.

Woods, David, and Frank O'Brien. Apollo 8 Flight Journal. NASA History Division, April 10, 2017. history.nasa.gov/afj/ap08fj/index.html.

IMAGE CREDITS

INDEX

Note: Page references in *italics* indicate photographs or illustrations.

abstract mathematics, 42
accelerometers, 100
Ada, Countess of Lovelace,
    115–17, *116*
Ada Lovelace Award, 117
Agnew, Spiro, *212*
agnosticism, 45
air defense, 83–84
Aldrin, Buzz, *183, 189*
    Apollo 11 mission, 192–93, 196, 202,
        204, 208, *209*
    Gemini flight, 186, *189*
    honored at state dinner, 211
    Presidential Medal of Freedom,
        212
American Indians, 6–9
Analytical Engine, 115–16
Anders, Bill, 173, 175, 177, 178–79,
    185
Apollo 1, 159–60, *160*
Apollo 1 crew patch, *158*
Apollo 8
    astronaut error, 178–79
    broadcast from lunar orbit, 177
    Earthrise photo from, *176*
    enter lunar orbit, 175–76
    flawless software performance, 191
    goal of, 173
    Lauren bug error, 181–85
    leaves low Earth orbit, 174
    star sightings, 173–74, *178*
Apollo 9, 192
Apollo 10, 192

Apollo 11
    astronauts, 192–93
    computer code printouts, *195*
    histories of, 210–11
    landing site, *204*
    launching, 196–97
    lunar module, *190*
    moon landing, 207–10
    testing software for, 194
    1202 code alarm, 197, 199–205,
        200
Apollo 13, 184–85, 221
Apollo 17, *214*, 215–17
Apollo Guidance Computer (AGC)
    on Apollo 8 mission, 173–79
    design challenges, 102
    erasable memory, 193
    fixed memory, 193, *194*
    fly-by-wire innovation, 111–12
    legacy of, 218
    magnetic cores, 193–94
    miles of wire, 193
    purpose of, 95, 108–10
    secretive aspects of, 119
    size of, xv, 95, *112*, 193
    software for (*See* onboard flight
        software)
    spacecraft parts, 109–11
    success of, 218
Apollo-Soyuz, 217–18
applied mathematics, 42
Arcadian Copper Mine, *20, 22*,
    22–25, *24*

Armstrong, Neil, *135, 183*
  Apollo 11 mission, 192, 196, *197,* 204,
    207–8
  honored at state dinner, 211
  knowledge and skills, 132
  Presidential Medal of Freedom, *212*
astronauts. *See also specific astronauts*
  adapt to idea of computers, 133–34
  on Apollo 1, *160*
  doubts about computers, xv–xvi, 132
  experts' confidence in, 211
  jet pilot backgrounds, 132–33
Auge Kugel method, 149–50, 184

Babbage, Charles, 115–16
Bacon, Deborah, 31–32
Bales, Steve, 200, *201,* 203, 211–12
Bartik, Jean Jennings, *68,* 68–69
Battin, Richard, 113–14, 157, 174, 213
binary code, 75
Black Friday, 154
Blair-Smith, Hugh, 160–61
Borman, Frank, 173, 175, 177, 183, *185*
Boston Globe newspaper, 93
Brandeis University, 63
Brooklyn Bridge, *56*
Bryn Mawr, 47, *47*
butterfly effect, *70,* 77–81

calculators, electronic, 188
Carpenter, Scott, *133*
Cassini, Jean-Dominique, 11
Chaffee, Roger, 160, *160*
chaos theory, 78
Civil Rights Act of 1964, 93
Cold War, 49–53, *84,* 96, 218
Collins, Mike, *183*
  Apollo 11 mission, 193, 196
  honored at state dinner, 211
  Presidential Medal of Freedom, *212*
command module (CM), *109,* 109–11,
    144, 225
command module (CM) simulator, *141*
communism, *48, 50,* 96
computer chips, 218
computer hackers, 88–89
computer programs. *See* software

computers. *See also* Apollo Guidance
    Computer
  in the 1950s, 61, *62*
  America's lead in, 218
  AN/FSQ-7 (Q7), 83–84
  electronic, introduction of, 62–63
  Honeywell 1800, *150*
  LGP-30, 72, *72,* 73–75
  PDP-1, 88–89
  treated as a toy, 88–89
  Whirlwind, 71
  XD-1, 83–84, *87*
copper, pure, *26*
copper mining, 18, *19, 23*

descent propulsion system (DPS), 125
Desk Set (movie), *60,* 62–63
dogmatism, 45
Draper, Charles Stark "Doc"
  on Air Force One, *103*
  British sports car, *105*
  dinner with Kennedy brothers,
    xi–xii
  hired for Project Apollo, 99, 103–4
  hosts celebratory dinner, 216–17, *217*
  lectures on engineering, *103*
  reaction to FORGET IT alarm, 126
  reaction to Project Apollo
    announcement, xiv
DSKY (display and keyboard), *106, 112,
    130, 197, 200*
  astronauts' interest in, 134–35
  description of, 113
  information on, 203–4

Earlham College, 30, 35–37, *36, 45, 57*
Earthrise, 176
emergency programs, 211
engineers, xv–xvi
ENIAC, *67,* 67–69, *68*
error detection and recovery in real time,
    137–42, 203, 211, 218
executive overflow alarm, 203

fail-safe mechanism, 140, 200
FORGET IT program, 123, 125–29, *127,*
    131

frictional heating, 177
funny little things (FLTs), 147

Galilei, Galileo, 193
Garman, Jack, 200–201, *201*, 205, 212
Gates, Bill, 220–21
Gavin, Joseph, 134
Gemini missions, 159, 186–88, *187*
Gibran, Kahlil, 167
Girton College, 46
Glenn, John, *133*
gravitational tug, 174
Great Depression, 4
Grissom, Gus, 160, *160*
gyroscope, 100

hackers, 88–89
Hamilton, David, *17*
Hamilton, Esther, 14, 16
Hamilton, Jim, *54*, 55–59, 64, *64*, 85
Hamilton, John, *17*
Hamilton, Kathryn, *17*
Hamilton, Kenneth, 14, 16, 19
Hamilton, Lauren, 64, *64*, 120, 156, *180*, 181
Hamilton, Margaret. *See also* Hamilton, Margaret (career)
  birth, 3
  childhood, 3–8, *5*, 13–18
  Earlham College years, *34*, 35–58, *38*
  early interest in math, 27
  generosity, 37–38
  high school years, *12*, *17*, 18–27
  homecoming queen, 19, *34*, 38, *38*
  insurance work, 61–63
  with Jim, *54*, *64*
  with Lauren, *64*, *180*
  legacy of, 220, 222
  marriage, 58
  Michigan college years, 30–33
  nonconformist nature, 37
Hamilton, Margaret (career)
  Ada Lovelace award, 117
  Apollo-Soyuz work, 217–18
  develops error detection and recovery program, 137–42
  Exceptional Space Act Award, 228

grueling working hours, 215
IL job interviews, 94–95
increasing responsibilities at IL, 131–32
initial IL assignments, 122–23
at Instrumentation Lab, *95*, *136*, *152*
lecture after Apollo, *206*
next to bound code books, *226*
next to command module, *225*
Presidential Medal of Freedom, 220, *221*
proudest accomplishment, 218–19
put in charge of all onboard flight software, 191–92
SAGE software work, 83–88
in SCAMA room, *175*, *216*
Skylab program, 217
starts a software company, 219
teaching job, 59
time line, 227–28
weather forecasting work, 64–65, 71–81
witnesses first launch, 215–16
at XD-1 control center, *82*
Hancock High School, 18–19
Hanks, Tom, 221
hardware, defined, 65
Heafield, Kenneth, *164*, 165–69, *168*, *169*
Heafield, Margaret "Bunny," 2, 3, 4. *See also* Hamilton, Margaret
Hiatt, Jean, 42
The Hobbit (Tolkien), 147
home economics, 16
Hopper, Grace, 221–22

inertial measurement unit (IMU), 100, 174
Instrumentation Lab (IL)
  contract for Apollo work, xiv, 99, 103–4, *104*
  headquarters, *90*, *120*, 120–21, *121*
  hired for Apollo contract work, *92*, 93–94
  interviews and hires Margaret, 94–95
  NASA pressure on, 153–56, 210
  office atmosphere, 119–20
  praise for software team, 218
  SCAMA room, 125, *126*, *175*, *182*, *216*

integrated circuits, 218
interface errors, 131

jet pilots, 132–33
job listings, 93
Johnson, Katherine, *143*, 143–45
Johnson, Lyndon B., *103*
Jordan, Michael, 221

Kennedy, John F., xi–xii, xi–xiv, *xiii*,
    96
Kennedy, Robert, xi–xii, *xiii*
Keystone View Company, 55–56
Kranz, Gene, *128*, 128–29

landing radar, 202
landmark tracking, *122*
Lauren bug, 181–85
Lincoln Lab, 85–88
Locke-Ober Café, xi–xii, *xiv*, xv, 134
logic, 43
Long, Florence, *40*, 41
Longfellow, Henry Wadsworth, 7
Lorenz, Edward, 71–79, *76*
Lorenz attractor, *70*
Lovell, Jim, *185*
    Apollo 8 mission, 173–74, 177, 178,
        178, 181, 182–85, 186
    played by Tom Hanks in movie, 221
lunar gravity, 175
lunar module (LM), *109*, 109–11, *111*,
    124, *138*, *190*, 202
lunar module (LM) simulator, *197*
lunar-orbit rendezvous, 110

magnetic cores, 193–94
Mariner 1, *146*, 148–49
Martin, Fred, 210
Massachusetts Institute of Technology
    (MIT), *121. See also* Instrumentation
    Lab
    academic reputation, 71
    Lincoln Lab, 85–88
mathematics, 27, 42
memory dump, 184
Merry-Go-Round bar, *86*
meteorology software, 64–65, 71–81

Michigan
    Lower Peninsula, *xviii*
    University of, *28*, 31–33, *32*
    Upper Peninsula, *xviii*, 3, 6–7, 7, 13
    winters, *4*, *167*
Michigan College of Mining and
    Technology, 7, *19*
military flying, 132–33
Milton, John, 193
Mission Control, *128*, *183*, *201*
    and Apollo 8 mission, 184
    and Apollo 11 mission, 197, 200,
        208–10
    and lunar module test flight, 125
    response to FORGET IT, 128
moon
    Apollo 11 landing site, *204*
    craters, *172*
    first landing on, 207–10, *209*
    landing program, xiii–xiv (*See also*
        Project Apollo)
    Moon Maiden, 9–10, *10*, *11*
    myths and legends, 8, 9–10
    telescopic map of, 10
    up close, *170*
music, 17–18

NASA. *See also* Mission Control
    places pressure on IL, 153–56, 210
    never-supposed-to-happen alarms,
        199–205
newspaper job listings, 93
Nixon, Richard, 211–12, *212*
Norton, John, 148–51, 221

Obama, Barack, 220, *221*
onboard flight software
    bound computer printouts, *151*, *195*,
        195–96, *226*
    creating priority display, 137–42
    FORGET IT program, 123, 125–29,
        127, 131
    Margaret hired for, 95
    Margaret's responsibility for, 191–92
    new hires for, 113–14
    reentry equation, 144–45, *145*
    size of, 153–54

time for testing and installation, 194
trimming code lines from, 154–55
what it does, xv
orbital rendezvous, 192–93

pacing item, 154
philosophy, 14–15, 43
pi (ratio), 149
Picket slide rule, 188, *188*
the Pleiades, *98*
poetry, 14–15, 166, 193
Presidential Medal of Freedom, *212*, 220, *221*
Presley, Elvis, 37, *52*, 52–53, 55
Principles and Practices for the Legal Secretary (Heafield), 166
priority display, 137–42, 199, *200*, 218
priority scheduling, 140–41, 203
PROG light, 199, *200*
Program 01, 181, 184
Project Apollo. *See also* Apollo Guidance Computer; onboard flight software
    contract with IL, xiv, 99
    formal announcement of, 99
    risk of mistakes, 137
    technical requirements, 100–102

Quakers, 35

realigning the inertial platform, 174
reentry to earth, 144–45, *145*, 177
religion, 15, 33, 44
rendezvous radar, 202, 210
rocket, Soviet, *97*
Root, E. Merrill, 49–53, 55
Ross, Diana, 221

SAGE (Semi-Automatic Ground Environment) air defense project, 83–84, 87–88
Saturn V rocket, 161–63, *162*
SCAMA room, 125, *126*, *175*, *182*, *216*
Scott, Charlotte Angas, 42, *46*, 46–47
Scott, David, 133
75 Cambridge Parkway, 119, *120*, 120–21

sexism
    and Civil Rights Act, 93
    on college campuses, 32
    in computer sciences, 85, 220, 222
    in male-only dining establishments, xii, xv
    in mathematics, 42–43, 46–47
    in schools, 17
    and working mothers, 64–65
sextant, 100, *101*
Shepard, Alan, *118*, *133*
Silver, George, 210
Skylab program, 217
Slayton, Deke, *133*
slide rules, 186–88, *188*, *189*
slipstick, 188
smoking, 57
software. *See also* onboard flight software
    Analytical Engine, 115–16
    defined, 107–8
    errors (bugs), 147–51
    origin of term, 65
    subroutines, 151
    taking photos of, 195–96
    Universal Systems Language, 219
software engineers, 116, 157
The Song of Hiawatha, 7–8
Soviet Union, xi, xiii, 49–53, 96, 218
space race, 96–97, 218
space travel, xi–xiv
Sputnik, *51*, 52–53
star sightings, 173–74, *178*, 182–83
statistics, 42
subroutines, 151
the Supremes, 221

telescope, 100, 193
Tindall, Howard W. "Bill," 154–55, *155*, 159, 218
tornadoes, *88*
Travelers Insurance Company, 61–63
A Trip Around the Moon (Verne), x
Trueblood, Elton, 43–44, *44*, 45, 58, 96
Tukey, John W., 65–66
1202 code alarm, 197, *198*, 199–205, *200*

Universal Systems Language, 219
University of Michigan, *28*, 31–33, *32*
Upper Peninsula (UP), *xviii*, 3, 6–7, *7*, 13
U.S. Air Force, 83

Walitalo, Arvo, *22*, 22–23, 25, 29
weather forecasting software, 71–81
Webb, James E., 99, *103*
White, Ed, 160, *160*
Woolworth, 21
World War II, 5–6